Affirmative Action and West Indian Intellectual Tradition

Affirmative Action and West Indian Intellectual Tradition

by

Ian Isidore Smart

Original World Press
Washington, D.C. and Port-of-Spain

Original World Press
55 Edward Street, Port-of-Spain
Trinidad & Tobago

P.O. Box 4578
Silver Spring, MD 20914-4578

www.iansmart.com

First Edition 2004

Printed in the United States of America

Library of Congress Control Number: 2003098385
ISBN 0-9641929-8-5

Cover art and layout by David Boothman

For

Mary Dawkins

My mother-in-law

Il ne faut pas neuf mois, il faut soixante ans pour faire un homme, soixante ans de sacrifices, de volonté, de ... de tant de choses! Et quand cet homme est fait, quand il n'y a plus en lui rein de l'enfance, ni de l'adolescence, quand vraiment, il est un homme, il n'est plus bon qu'à mourir.

ANDRÉ MALRAUX, *LA CONDITION HUMAINE*

CONTENTS

INTRODUCTION

Attibon Legba
Attibon Legba
Ouvri bayi pou' moi
HAITIAN INVOCATION

Papa Legba leads us to confront the cardinal contradictions of our human condition not with nihilistic cynicism but with laughter, warm, rich laughter, laughter that heals. An enslaved African of advanced years and the corresponding wisdom was once accosted by the young white man who was the first born of the owner of a large plantation in South Carolina. Hostilities had just begun and the young man was resplendent in a brand-new Confederate first lieutenant's uniform.

"How do I look?" the young man enquired of the gray-haired African dressed in the coarse ill-fitting rags of the enslaved.

"Like a lion," replied the subservient serf, rolling his eyes in that characteristic "Negro" expression of admiration.

The young white man patronizingly reminded his inferior that he was born right there on the plantation and had never traveled to Africa. It was patently obvious, then, that the African had never laid eyes on any of those fabled animals. The old African responded with fawning insistence that he had, indeed, seen a lion, right there tethered in the field.

The young white man, understanding the profound intellectual limitations of the darker race, generously and in the simple language best suited for communication with "Negroes," pointed out that the referenced animal was not a lion but a jackass.

That wise old African had followed the counsel of Papa Legba. Human civilization is now faced with one of its greatest crises. Might has made itself right in an entirely unprecedented manner. However, Papa Legba leads us to laughter not to despair. Certainly, the antics of the neo-conservatives and fundamentalists on both sides of the massive ideological divide inspire laughter. The image of the commander-in-chief resplendent in the regalia of a warrior pilot calls to mind the tale of the young plantation owner and his African servant, and has generated incessant laughter. So, too, have the analogously fanciful press releases emanating from the Iraqi Ministry of Information right up to the fall of Baghdad in April 2003 C.E.

According to Henry Louis Gates, Jr., Papa Legba is the Yoruba deity who is the model for the African American mythical Signifying Monkey. And, according to the African American tradition, "Signifying is a nigger's occupation." The title of this book contains two terms, "Affirmative Action" and "West Indian," each susceptible to various interpretations that may be mutually exclusive. The terms lend themselves, then, to the kind of wordplay which constitutes a fundamental form of signifying.

White supremacy emerged as an organized system only at the beginning of the nineteenth century. However, the societies created in the Americas consequent on the arrival of Columbus were certainly founded on the principle of white male privilege. This privilege constituted and still constitutes an entitlement, for it is a benefit bestowed to members of a specified group, and not an earned benefit. This principle is the first form of affirmative action. In the 1960s, the greatly revered President John F. Kennedy is said to have been the initiator of an Affirmative Action policy which proved to be the model for the federal government of the United States in its programmatic response to the Civil Rights Movement.

Kennedy, a white man born with a gold spoon in his mouth, was thus intimately familiar with bedrock affirmative action. Since white supremacy is based on the erosion of the self-respect of the nonwhite, for the oppressed, self-affirmation (generally referred to as self-determination) is the necessary and sufficient condition for liberation. The interplay of the various acceptations of "affirmative" and "affirmation" is employed in this book to enhance the reader's understanding of the issues discussed.

In the interest of clarity and consistency, when the term Affirmative Action is used with upper case "A," it refers exclusively to the Affirmative Action Program instituted by the federal government of the United States as a consequence of the Civil Rights Movement. When the term affirmative action is used with lower case "a," it references exclusively the system of affirmative action as white male privilege/entitlement. This system is the bedrock of all societies developed in North, South, and Central America, with the exception of post-revolutionary Haiti and the other societies created by Africans who had liberated themselves from white supremacy.

The term "West Indian" is the preferred self-designation of those self-engaged inhabitants of the English-speaking Caribbean who consider themselves to be different from, and better than, so-called "Black Americans." The term is deliberately chosen for the title of this book in order to signify on those who consider "West Indians" to be essentially different from Africans born in the United States. The representative West Indian intellectual presented in this book is an African who happened to have been born in the Anglophone Caribbean. Since he is essentially African, the differences between his cultural tradition and the African American cultural tradition are merely accidental.

Following the lead of Papa Legba, we have tried to avoid bitterness and contention. So much confusion abounds, and it is the work of the true intellectual to help readers clear a path through the thick undergrowth of deliberate distortions, misunderstandings, groundless fears, and prejudices. This is a path which would lead us out of the jungle, the Bush if you will, to the centers of civilized existence.

The ancient Africans from Kemet were the first humans to proclaim the power of the word. The Memphite Theology, a document written in remote antiquity but which was edited over and over again during the many millennia of Kemetic history, opens with the declaration: "The Primate of the Gods, Ptah, conceived in his heart, everything that exists and by His utterance created them all" (*Stolen Legacy* 139). For these ancient Africans, Ptah is one of the three persons of the Triune God. The other two are Ra and Amen. Few and far between are the scholars who acknowledge the Memphite Theology as the source of the New Testament text: "In the beginning was the Word and the Word was with God, and the Word was God" (John 1:1).

The path out of confusion can be created only through a redefinition of terms. The main contribution of this text book, then, will be a new understanding of fundamental terms employed in contemporary public discourse. A new perspective on generally accepted notions will be offered, and, necessarily, new definitions of old terms will be presented. We will do so in the tradition of African wisdom literature, in the spirit of the first book ever written by any human being, *The Teachings of Ptahhotep* (published between 2388 and 2356 B.C.). This is the tradition of Papa Legba.

Opponents have sought to dismiss the bulk of our work as "self-published." This present book will be particularly objectionable to these detractors, because its approach is so overtly self-centered. For I have presented myself as a representative West Indian intellectual. It is impossible to conceive of any spirituality system which is not centered on what Saint Paul proclaims to be the two fundamental commandments: to love God above all things and to love the Other as much as we love the Self.

The Honorable Marcus Mosiah Garvey, an authentic West Indian, enjoined on Africans that they "do for self." Self-publishing is the most basic form of self-affirmation for any African intellectual. Self-publishing is, then, the primary manifestation of self-love for the African intellectual. The self-love envisioned by Saint Paul is fundamentally self-centered. Self-centeredness is the basis of self-preservation for the African intellectual as for every being. The authentic West Indian intellectual is African in the fullest sense of the term. Bob Marley, another authentic West Indian, called upon Africans throughout the world to liberate themselves from mental slavery. We, therefore, are particularly pleased and proud that white supremacists would seek to dismiss our work as "self-published."

CHAPTER ONE

Setting the Record Straight

I want to be real with you.
FABOLOUS

AS used in the title of this book, the term "Affirmative Action" refers only to that program set up by the federal government of the United States of North America as a direct result of the Civil Rights Movement of the 1960s. Furthermore, as used in the title of this book, the term is further limited to that part of the program which relates to higher education. The term "Affirmative Action" is then to have as its referent the Affirmative Action Program in higher education.

The term "West Indian" carries much baggage, and progressive scholars prefer to replace it with "Caribbean." However, for the purposes of this book, the problematic and perhaps dated designation is preferable. In the Anglophone Caribbean, the term "West Indian" has been used to designate the inhabitants of the English-speaking islands and mainland territories. The principal mainland territories have been the Republic of Guyana in South America and Belize in Central America. However, there are significant population groups in the Spanish-speaking Central

American nations of Panama, Costa Rica, and Nicaragua who identify themselves as West Indian, for they are the progeny principally of immigrants from the Anglophone islands. As will be discussed later on in this chapter, the designation "Garifuna" is reserved for the descendants of the earliest wave of immigrants. The majority of the Garifuna people now live in Honduras and Belize (formerly British Honduras).

The author of this book is presented as the representative West Indian intellectual. There are compelling reasons for this: the author is a legitimate West Indian; he is a legitimate intellectual; and he, clearly, is the West Indian intellectual with whose experience the author is most familiar.

Howard University and the Afrocentric Intellectual

Will Mercer Cook is one of the shining lights of the African American scholarly tradition. He came from a distinguished Washington D.C. Negro family and was born on March 30, 1903 in the Federal District. His grandfather had been secretary to the white military man who in 1867 founded Howard University, General Oliver Otis Howard. The university is the Capstone of those historically black colleges and universities (HBCUs), which the white supremacist federal government of the United States created right after the end of the Civil War to meet the higher education needs of the nation's newest citizens, the emancipated "Negroes." Cook's father was born on the campus of Howard University.

Cook is, then, the quintessential Howard University intellectual. He was one of those fortunate "Negroes" selected to pursue a first-rate education in the mainstream Eurocentric academic system. Although he received his primary and secondary training at the premiere Negro schools of Washington, D.C., he did not attend the Capstone of Negro education but rather one of the most prestigious white institutions of higher learning, Amherst College. There, in 1925, he received his B.A. "Negroes" who were anointed by the mainstream system were typically permitted to pursue all of their studies at the very best universities. Of course, such anointed "Negroes" have always been carefully chosen and are expected to adhere faithfully to the canons. Cook, therefore, took his M.A. and Ph.D. in French at Brown University, completing the terminal degree in 1936.

For fourteen years, Cook headed the Department of Romance Languages at Howard University. He finally retired in 1970. He died of pneumonia on October 4, 1987 at the Washington Hospital Center. Cook had been converted to Roman Catholicism as an adult, and his funeral services were held at the Sacred Heart Catholic church in the heart of the Latino section of the nation's capital. The author of this book, the representative West Indian intellectual, was one of those who went to pay last respects to this great Howard University humanist.

At the time of Will Mercer Cook's funeral, the West Indian intellectual was a full professor of Spanish in the Department of Romance Languages at the Capstone. Having first come to Howard as an assistant professor of Spanish in 1977, his tenure had never coincided with Cook's. The West Indian intellectual considers Cook to be the most distinguished intellectual to have served as a professor of Modern Languages at the Capstone of "Negro" Education.

Cook turned out to be a committed African-centered intellectual. He thus opted for a different path from the one prescribed for anointed "Negroes." He joined forces with Langston Hughes to translate one of the most important Haitian novels of the twentieth century, *Gouverneurs de la rosée*, by the Haitian, Jacques Roumain. Two African Americans, one a master bard of the Harlem Renaissance, the other a master of the French language, combined their efforts to make one of the finest Caribbean novels of the 20th century available to the Anglophone world. The product is the artistic English language version entitled *Masters of the Dew*, published by Collier Books of New York in 1971.

Moving in the same vein, Cook made his most significant contribution to Academe with his editing and translation of a collection of writings by the Senegalese intellectual, Cheikh Anta Diop. This work, entitled *The African Origin of Civilization: Myth or Reality*, was published in 1976 by Lawrence Hill of New York. It was the first English language version of Diop's groundbreaking scholarship. *Masters of the Dew* established an important bridge between the African American and the Caribbean intellectual traditions. *The African Origin of Civilization* not only bridged the great divide between the African American scholar and his counterpart in Mother Africa, but it provided the most important intellectual base for the Afrocentric movement. Since Cook's scholarly work went beyond the limits imposed by the mainstream, his two most important books were not published by any university press, but rather by commercial presses.

Molefi Kete Asante's *Afrocentricity* (Buffalo, New York: Amulefi, 1980) is generally considered to be the defining text of the Afrocentric movement. Those who accept without question the premises of the Eurocentric academic system would be inclined to dismiss Asante's watershed work as "self-published." Asante is an African American, and his contribution stands on the work of pioneers such as Diop, who was not an African American.

Another of these pioneers was George G. M. James, who was born in what was then British Guiana and came to the United States to study. He taught mathematics, Latin, and Greek at a number of HBCUs in the South. In 1954, he self-published *Stolen Legacy,* with the intriguing subtitle: *The Greeks were not the authors of Greek Philosophy, but the people of North Africa commonly called the Egyptians*. The main thesis of *Stolen Legacy* is precisely that of *The African Origin of Civilization.* Whereas James's research is limited to Greco-Roman literature, Diop was a trained scientist as well as a linguist, a uniquely qualified Egyptologist, since he was a native speaker of several African languages.

Asa G. Hilliard, an African born in the United States is a contemporary Afrocentric scholar of great repute. He is the Fuller E. Calloway Professor of Education at Georgia State University, Atlanta. Since he holds an endowed chair in a white university, he would be deemed by the mainstream Academy to be a preeminent scholar. In his introduction to the 1985 reprint of *Stolen Legacy* Hilliard declares:

> Mental bondage is invisible violence. . . .
>
> Creators and beneficiaries of belief systems develop a vested interest in the system, to the extent that they become conscious of it as a system. Actions are taken to nurture and to maintain the controlling system intact. Competing belief systems come to be regarded as "pagan," "heretical," "disloyal," and so forth. "Priests" or "professors" are "ordained" or "certified" as purveyors of the system, sometimes with the belief that they are "objective" and "scientific." The general public usually accepts and comes to depend upon the "doctrine" or "knowledge." When an occasional scholar, priest, or member of the general public discovers new questions and new treatments of information, especially informa-

> tion that challenges the bedrock of the belief and thinking system, that person is frequently met with silence, denial, isolation, even death.

Afrocentric scholarship promotes paradigm shift. It fundamentally challenges the established order, the canon. And the established order, the system, true to itself, wages relentless war against this disquieting challenge. The Academy defines its position as "objective" and "scientific." Those who dare take issue with the accepted notions, the dogmas, are maligned as "ideologues," "controversial," "polemical."

Hilliard continues:

> The reception of Professor James' book has been less than enthusiastic. Published in 1954, it has been virtually out of circulation since that time. There are no reviews in the standard places, no promotions and advertising, and if the scholarly establishment is aware of it at all, it is virtually unquoted.

The cold shoulder awaits any scholar presenting fresh new ideas which challenge the status quo. Thus every truly Afrocentric scholar will have his work suffer the same fate as James's. He will be hard put to be deemed preeminent by the accepted spokesmen of the established academic system.

Diop's voice is the most authoritative in the field of Afrocentric studies, and Diop steadfastly directs scholars to turn to Kemet (Egypt) for a proper understanding of the development of human civilization. Consequent on the invasion of Iraq and the pillaging of its cultural heritage, there has been much talk of Mesopotamia as the "cradle of civilization." Diop's voice, reaching out through Cook's translation, emphatically declares:

> Thus, it is in Egypt that we encounter, with mathematical certainty, humanity's most ancient historical date [4241 B.C. (4236 after a slight correction of the first calculations)]. What do we find in Mesopotamia? Nothing susceptible of being dated with certainty. . . .
>
> Egypt's pyramids, temples, and obelisks, its abundance of columns at Luxor and Karnak, its avenues of Sphinxes, the colossi of Memnon, its rock carvings, its underground temples with proto-Doric columns (Deir-el-Bahari) at Thebes, are an architectural reality still palpable today, historical evidence that no dogma can blow into thin air. In contrast, what did Iran (Elam) and Mesopotamia produce prior to the eighth century (epoch of the Assyrians)? Only shapeless clay mounds. (100-01)

Hilliard's great work in Afrocentric scholarship includes the editing of a translation of the Prisse Papyrus under the title of *The Teachings of Ptahhotep*. The zealous defenders of Eurocentric privilege in Academe might scornfully dismiss this important work by Hilliard as "self-published."

In his introduction to the *The Teachings*, Hilliard explains that a French explorer removed a document from a tomb of an eleventh dynasty Pharoah. This document "was eighteen pages of papyrus on which near perfect hieratic writing was found" (6). Fourteen pages of the document contained the complete work of a certain Ptahhotep.

> There is a tomb for Ptahhotep near the Step Pyramid in the cemetery at Sakkara. Many authorities believe, and the strongest evidence supports the belief, that he was the Ptahhotep who was the author of the book. . . . Ptahhotep himself was said to be the eldest legitimate son of an unnamed Pharaoh, and was 110 years old when he wrote his book. (7)

It is estimated that Ptahhotep wrote this book sometime between 2388 B.C. and 2356 B.C. This wise man from ancient Africa is therefore, as far as our knowledge goes, the first human being to write a book.

The Eurocentric Academy presents as one of its dogmas that the Greeks were the first to engage in the activity we label philosophy. It is an unquestioned assumption that humankind's earliest philosophers were the Greeks of the Ionian School: Thales, Anaximander, and Anaximenes. These men reached their prime in the sixth century B.C. If the Affirmative Action Program as we understand it today means anything, it would mean working to liberate African Americans and, indeed, all Americans from the darkness of mental bondage. Affirmative Action would mean setting the record straight. It would mean correcting the egregious inconsistency of attributing to the Greeks who lived in the sixth century B.C. the achievement of founding humankind's scholarly and literary tradition.

James shows over and over again how fantasies and falsehoods pass as facts in the field of the history of civilization. Aristotle, who lived in the fourth century B.C. could not have authored the hundreds of books attributed to him. It is claimed that he was a pupil of Plato, who was a moral philosopher. It is implausible that he would have spent twenty years studying under Plato who knew only moral philosophy. It is more likely that Aristotle spent his formative years as a guest of Alexander in Egypt. There, he would have culled all of his knowledge from the rich tradition of scholarship which, without any doubt, had existed in Egypt for at least three millennia prior to Alexander's arrival.

One of the dogmas handed down by canonical Academe holds African literature to be quintessentially oral. The team of

Howard University scholars who designed the core Introduction to the Humanities course created in 1993 a document reflecting their understanding of the humanities. In it, they declare the original humanists to be those scholars of the Italian and English Renaissance who reemphasized "the centrality of the *litterae humaniores,* or classical literature, history, and moral philosophy to their educational system and worldview" (2). "Centrality" is taken uncritically as chronological primacy, and it is assumed that mankind's first great written literary expression emerged in Greece. Indeed, the Howard University document appears to accept without question this assumption and so focuses on the African oral literary tradition, presenting it as that continent's fundamental contribution to the humanities.

James P. Allen, a contemporary white Egyptologist, in *Middle Egyptian: An Introduction to the Language and Culture of Hieroglyphs,* offers a brief but powerful essay on Egyptian literature. Allen declares:

> The Egyptians were also aware of the difference between ordinary conversation or writing and the kind of carefully crafted language that we call literature. The latter was known as *mdwt nfrt* "beautiful speech" (much like the French term *belles lettres*) . . . It is a nice reflection on Egyptian society that the possession of this talent was not felt to be limited to the upper classes or the educated. One of the most famous pieces of Egyptian literature is a series of discourses on the nature of Maat, expounded by a peasant from one of the oases (the "boondocks" of ancient Egypt); and another text tells us that "Beautiful speech is more hidden than gemstones, yet it is found with servant-women at the millstones." (241)

Scholars and, indeed, the general public have no problems

acknowledging the creative genius of the oral poets, and so-called "folk" musicians, artisans, artists, sculptors found in every African community. However, it would come as a great surprise to these scholars, as well as to the general public, to be informed that from the very beginning of recorded history, African civilization has considered literature, and this refers to scribal as well as oral literature, to be the province of common folk, and even of servant-women. The general public and the scholarly community are blissfully unaware that the first book ever written by a known author was the work of a learned priest of Kemet.

On the basis of this information, the truly objective scholar will feel the moral obligation to revise accepted notions about the humanities and the classics. To undertake this revision is not to be "polemical," rather it is to be truly scientific. The pursuit of the true facts might be deemed to be an "obsession." However, what truly significant intellectual in the history of humanity did not engage in the pursuit of an obsession. Some sciolists have judged Afrocentric scholars to be "ideological," as if scholarship itself were not inherently ideological.

Clarifying the Notion of Affirmative Action

The historical background is presented in this book not just to glorify the past, but to counter the prevailing falsehoods. It is accepted as self-evident that the Greeks invented civilization. It is accepted as self-evident that no great civilizations ever arose in Africa. It is accepted as a given that it took European colonization to bring light to the dark continent. The West Indian intellectual's *Amazing Connections: Kemet to Hispanophone Africana Litera-*

ture challenged these unproven assumptions with respect to Hispanic culture and civilization. The same assumptions regarding the origin of Carnival were questioned in *Ah Come Back Home: Perspectives on the Trinidad and Tobago Carnival.* It would have been foolhardy to attempt a discussion of the issue of Affirmative Action without first having made the preceding clarifications.

Affirmative Action as white privilege has always been the cornerstone of New World societies. In the final decade of the fifteenth century, the King and Queen of Castile and Aragon had the foresight to hire the Italian mercenary navigator to find new territories and a new route to the lucrative trading grounds of Asia. The established route at that time passed through territories controlled by Islamic infidels (the same lands of Northeast Africa which are generally called today, the Middle East). Thus it was that the two most important kingdoms of the land known today as Spain, having first consolidated into one through the politically brilliant maneuver of the marriage between Ferdinand and Isabel, won in 1492 the biggest colonial prize of all times, the entire Western Hemisphere.

The Portuguese, who had initiated the frenzy of conquest, were sore losers and appealed to Pope Alexander V1 to divvy up the spoils somewhat more equitably. Alexander was a Borja of the Spanish branch. He was born in Valencia, Spain. As the ruler of the Vatican he was obliged to be fair, so, through the instrument of the Treaty of Tordesillas, concluded in 1494, the spoils were more or less evenly divided between the two European nations.

It was argued in *Amazing Connections* that Spain and even Portugal were just barely European. It was not until 1492 that the last African Islamic kingdom, Granada, fell to the forces of the combined Spanish Christian kingdoms under the leadership of the

King and Queen of Castile and Aragon. Although the Portuguese had reconquered their territory from the invading Moors in the thirteenth century, they, like the peoples of Spain, having been lifted out of semi-barbarism by the conquering Moors, were indelibly marked by the African cultural tradition.

Of course, by the end of the sixteenth century other European nations were circling in on the rich booty. The English, the French, and the Dutch took over from the Spanish and Portuguese as the prime colonizing peoples. The new colonizing nations followed exactly the same template, one having as its basis affirmative action, white privilege, but for upper-class males. In the beginning the upper class were the nobility. However, in England and Holland, merchants established a firm place for themselves at the top of the societal pyramid. It took the French revolution to confirm definitively the ascendancy of the French bourgeoisie over the nobility. The American Revolution was an intellectual child of the French one, although it predated it by twenty-three years.

The spirit of the French revolution informed all of the New World societies which evolved after the so-called Age of Enlightenment. In South and Central America, new republics emerged based on the model of the United States. In all of these societies, affirmative action for ruling class white males continued to be the cornerstone. In the islands of the Caribbean, the primitive colonial system remained in place. The fact that the slave-owning whites were now more of the bourgeoisie than the nobility made little difference to the majority of the population. It is only in Haiti that a true popular revolution occurred, replacing the white bourgeoisie/nobility ruling class with an African ruling elite. The Haitian Revolution, completed in 1804, is thus the only authentic New World revolution.

The British, ever the pragmatists, were the first of the colonial powers to terminate the system of chattel slavery. They discovered that free labor on their West Indian plantations would be more profitable. They abolished slavery in 1833 but callously obliged the enslaved Africans to remain on the plantations for five more years. This was done as part of the reparation package given to the slave-owning whites.

Even during the period of enslavement of Africans, the British understood the wisdom of indoctrinating a few select Africans. One of these was a certain Francis Williams, whose biography is presented in the overtly patronizing study penned by Henri Grégoire, *An Enquiry Concerning the Intellectual and Moral Faculties and Literature of Negroes: Followed with an Account of the Life and Works of Fifteen Negroes and Mulattoes Distinguished in Science, Literature and the Arts.* D. B. Warden authored the English translation, which was published in Brooklyn in 1810.

Grégoire reports that Williams was born in Jamaica of African parents sometime around the end of the seventeenth century. His precocious intelligence impressed the colonial governor of the island, who decided to play God with the child, sending him off to England to be educated as if he were a white youth of the ruling class. Williams attended private schools and finally took a degree in Latin and mathematics at Cambridge. Grégoire adopts an authorial approach consonant with that of the arrogant colonial governor and reports with ill-concealed satisfaction that Williams returned to the island a fish out of water. "He described himself to be a white man with black skin, for he despised men of colour, and often said, shew me a Negro, and I'll show you a thief" (210).

After they were forced to dismantle the slave system, the British found it even more important to train some of the inferior people to act as "white men with black skin." The preference would have been first for the mulatto types, however, there were not enough of these to meet the need. Thus within one generation of the abolition of slavery in the British West Indies, there began to emerge African intellectuals.

Self-Affirmation and West Indian Intellectual Tradition

John Jacob Thomas is an example of a West Indian intellectual who practiced the highest form of self-affirmation. He was born in 1840 in Central Trinidad, the heart of the colony's plantation belt. His parents would have been released from the vicious servitude on the plantation just two years before his birth. And they, as did the vast majority of the Africans who had been victims of the trans-Atlantic slave trade, reconnected with their traditions as soon as the opportunity presented itself. The data properly interpreted show that Africans who were subjected to the greatest crime against humanity persistently understood that luck is the confluence of opportunity and preparation. Thomas's parents understood that education, even though this was essentially an indoctrination into the white supremacist system, was the best preparation possible.

The British had seized Trinidad from Spain in 1799. However, at that time the Spanish Crown had already, through the agency of a treaty (the *Cédula de Población*) signed in 1783, initiated the process of large scale migration of Europeans and enslaved Africans to the island. The British honored this process, so that the vast majority of the population of the island at the time of Thomas's birth were French-Creole-speaking Africans. Thomas was therefore fluent in French Creole and English. Since he was a man who valued education, he was also fluent in French and proficient in Latin and Greek. His intellectual curiosity would have led him to master Spanish as well. Thomas dedicated his life to the liberation of his people through the dissemination of knowledge. He understood that knowledge is power.

In 1869, Thomas published his first book, *The Theory and Practice of Creole Grammar.* The publishers were The Chronicle Publishing Office of Port-of-Spain, Trinidad. The Chronicle was a newspaper, so Thomas's book was "self-published." Of course, at that time, even in the centers of Western civilization most books would have been self-published. Thomas prepared this book as a tool for liberating his people; for, as a school teacher, he would have found that all of his students spoke French Creole. The back cover of the 1969 reprint of Thomas's book declares:

> Thomas was one of the first anywhere to make a study of Creole, recognising this as a new and important developing language. It was a marriage of French and African forms — a parallel, as he thought, to 'the development of the Romance languages from their Latin stem after the Roman empire had broken up and barbarian peoples had begun to remould Latin according to their own verbal rhythms.'

Thomas clearly was engaged in paradigm shift, in challenging the accepted notions of African inferiority. He dared to equate Creole languages with Romance languages.

It is particularly significant that exactly a hundred years after its first publication, the book would have been reissued by New Beacon Books. John La Rose, a Trinidadian intellectual, is the moving force behind New Beacon Books. He created this entity precisely to give voice to those who had been locked out of the mainstream publishing houses consecrated by the scholarly establishment. La Rose understands that freedom of the press is only guaranteed to those who own one. La Rose is one of Thomas's direct progeny. Both are exemplars of the principle dear to Marcus Garvey, "do for self."

Gertrud Buscher in her introduction to the 1969 edition of Thomas's first book asserts:

> If John Jacob Thomas's name appears in most books on the history of Trinidad, however, it is not as the author of the first work on Trinidad Creole. It appears inevitably linked with that of James Anthony Froude, the English historian. (v)

Froude was one of those white supremacist mainstream ideologues who "had come to the West Indies early in 1887 on a tour of inspection." Within a year, the mainstream publishing establishment had converted Froude's racist ravings into a book entitled *The English in the West Indies* or *The Bow of Ulysses*. Buscher describes this book as "a work which left little doubt about his contempt for the majority of the inhabitants of the West Indies, for whom he felt that the status of crown colonies was the only suitable form of government" (v).

Froude was apparently dispatched to the West Indies by the British colonial masters to make short shrift of the thrust towards self-determination through constitutional reform, to which the majority African population had been dedicating their energies. This thrust was a manifestation of the visceral rejection of enslavement, which Africans had always evinced. Indeed, contrary to the doctrine taught by the mainstream academic system, slavery was not abolished as a result of an awakening of conscience on the part of whites. It was the Africans' unrelenting and visceral opposition to the greatest crime against humanity which finally forced the whites to abolish the system, when it ceased to be financially viable.

The book, *Ah Come Back Home: Perspectives on the Trinidad and Tobago Carnival*, maintains that the festival known as Carnival continues to serve as one of the most important engines driving the thrust of Trinidad and Tobago Africans towards total liberation from the white supremacist system. Certainly, during the Carnival celebrations of 1881, Africans in Port-of-Spain forced the colonial administration to repeal its restrictions on their festival. The common people inspired by their commitment to their cultural legacy engaged the police in pitched battles during the predawn Carnival Monday activities.

It is clear that Thomas partook of the same spirit which led his people to confront the might of the colonial regime on that Carnival Monday morning in 1881. Buscher reports as follows:

> There was much criticism and mockery of Froude, but none more eloquent than that of John Jacob Thomas. Summing up his judgement of Froude's writing in one word, *Froudacity*, Thomas not only came to the defense of the men of his race, but took the opportunity to launch an attack: if things had not always gone well in Trinidad, this was not the result of any innate inferiority of the black man, but could be explained very largely by the inept and corrupt personnel — from governors down the line — sent out by the Colonial Office. (vi)

With the clever wordplay which Africans from the beginning of recorded history have always demonstrated, it is Thomas who makes short shrift of Froude's mendacity, audacity, and intellectual fraud. Froude's work is nothing but "Froudacity." Thomas totally dismisses the rantings of the racist, "signifiying on him" (in African American parlance), "mamaguying him" (in Trinidad and Tobago parlance), "*mamagallándolo*" (in Afro-Hispanic parlance).

What is even more instructive are the actions taken by Thomas to ensure the efficacy of his attack on the white supremacist. Buscher recounts:

> Thomas was eager that his views should get attention by being published in England. He sold some lands he possessed in the south of the island, and despite 'mental tribulation' and ill-health — he had been suffering from what appears to have been tuberculosis for twelve years — he traveled to London in 1889. His book came out in the summer of that year and was received with great interest. (vi)

It can reasonably be assumed that Thomas used personal funds to finance the publication of his first book in 1869. This book was printed by the local newspaper press. However, for the attack on Froude, the agent of the Colonial Office, Thomas deemed it necessary to have the book published in the very capital of the empire. This enterprise required an extraordinary expenditure, perhaps of all of his personal wealth.

Thomas took the concept of self-publication to its ultimate limit. He succeeded in having his work, *Froudacity, West Indian Fables by James Anthony Froude—Explained by J. J. Thomas, Author of 'The Creole Grammar* , published in London in the summer of 1889. Not only was the work "self-published," but it was clearly "ideological" and "polemical." It was, nevertheless, received with great interest. And an American edition was issued the following year. Buscher reports:

> He was working on a revised edition when, no doubt largely as a

> result of his journey, the state of his health deteriorated, and the mail-boat arriving in Trinidad on 18th October, 1889, brought with it the news that John Jacob Thomas had died in London four weeks earlier. (vi)

Thomas literally gave up his life for the liberation of his people. And he saw this liberation as being effected through the self-publication of his books.

Wilfred Cartey is the individual who provided the firmest link between the West Indian intellectual tradition, the Capstone, and the author of this book. Cartey, born in Trinidad and Tobago, was educated under the British colonial system and came to the United States to pursue higher studies, completing the doctorate at Columbia University. He was a specialist in Romance languages as is the author of this book.

There is a half of a generation difference between Cartey and the West Indian intellectual. They came, however, from identical social circles. Cartey's older sister was a close friend of one of the West Indian intellectual's aunts. And one of the West Indian intellectual's uncles, a school teacher of sterling reputation in Trinidad and Tobago, was Cartey's earliest mentor. Cartey was a role model for the West Indian intellectual, especially when the latter came to the Capstone. Cartey understood the vital role the Capstone could play in emancipating Africans from white supremacy. And it was his enthusiasm which helped the West Indian intellectual to stay the course when the latter's dream of coming to teach at the Capstone had turned into a nightmare.

Although Cartey was not a member of the faculty of the Department of Romance Languages, he was a frequent visitor to the Capstone and served as a mentor not only to the West Indian intellectual, but to most of the faculty members, including Martha K. Cobb, an African American scholar who served as chair of the Department.

Basil Matthews was born in Trinidad and Tobago. He belonged to the same generation as the parents of the West Indian intellectual. Matthews' sister was the godmother of one of the West Indian intellectual's brothers. Matthews had served as one the earliest directors of the African Studies Department at the Capstone. By the time the West Indian intellectual began his tenure, however, Matthews had already retired. The West Indian intellectual, considering Matthews a venerable elder and family friend, established contact with him as soon as he arrived in Washington, D.C. These social ties were maintained up to Matthews' passing on to the Kingdom of the Ancestors.

C. L. R. James is deemed to be one of the great West Indian intellectuals of the twentieth century. Like Matthews he once served as director of the African Studies Department. James was born in Trinidad and Tobago in 1903, so that by 1977 he lived in glorified retirement. The author of this book was privileged to have James accede to his invitation to have dinner at his Takoma Park apartment in the spring of 1978. The most memorable pearl of wisdom dispensed by James on that occasion was the prediction that change would come to South Africa with lightning speed. James reminded his young host that in London of the 1930s African independence seemed a pipe dream. By 1945, however, the intellectual and even the political establishment were no longer scoffing at the idea.

Eric Eustace Williams was the first prime minister of the independent nation of Trinidad and Tobago, the land of his birth. Williams was born in 1911, won an island scholarship, and went to read history at Oxford. Francis Williams graduated from Cambridge in the early eighteenth century, preceding Eric by about two centuries. Things had changed greatly when Eric completed his studies, for now there were HBCUs. Indeed, Eric followed the tradition established by Cook, Alain Leroy Locke, and many others, that of bringing to the Capstone the indoctrination gained at the most prestigious universities of the Western world.

The British Colonial Educational System

The British Colonial Educational system in the West Indies was designed to train a few good natives—1 percent or less—to advance unquestioningly the interests of white supremacy. The vast majority of the natives were to be trained to read and write so as to be more efficient laborers. With the establishment of the HBCUs the North American whites sought to be more generous to their "Negroes." For the Negro colleges and universities were designed to give a tertiary education to the talented tenth—that is, the top ten percent of the inferior race.

This tertiary education was a Negro one, separate and unequal to that offered by the mainstream academic system. However, the white ruling class did permit a handful of Negroes, the upper, upper, upper crust—1 percent or less—to enter the hallowed halls of their most prestigious universities and colleges. In this, the British colonial system coincided exactly with the program set up by the federal government after the Civil War.

V. S. Naipaul, the renowned Trinidad and Tobago writer who won the Nobel Prize for literature in 1999, is a perfect example of the native admitted into the upper circles of the British academic system. He writes in *The Middle Passage: The Caribbean Revisited*:

> I knew Trinidad to be unimportant, uncreative, cynical. The only professions were those of law and medicine, because there was no need for any other; and the most successful people were commission agents, bank managers and members of the distributive trades. Power was recognized, but dignity was allowed to no one. Every person of eminence was held to be crooked and contemptible. We lived in a society which denied itself heroes. (43)

The truth hurts, but it must be faced. Naipaul was on target in his assessment of colonial society in Trinidad. It may be argued that even today, after four decades of "independence," things still remain basically the same. Indeed, the wickedly insightful commentary on Trinidad could be applied to any society of people who have accepted their inferior status. African Americans, like the majority of Africans on the globe, have accepted themselves as inferior. In general, it could, then, be claimed that in contemporary African American society: "Every person of eminence [is] held to be crooked and contemptible." Thus, in general, African Americans live "in a society which [denies] itself heroes."

Continuing in his corrosive commentary Naipaul declares:

> For talent, a futility, the Trinidadian substituted intrigue . . . Admiration he did have: for boys who did well at school, such academic success, separate from everyday life, giving self-respect to the community as a whole without threatening it in any way; for scholarship winners until they became conceited; for racehorses. And for cricketers. (44)

The scholarship winners were those natives who followed the footsteps of Francis Williams. Mercer Cook would be the United States equivalent of the scholarship winner, as would most of those "Negroes" who prior to the 1960s were admitted into the hallowed halls of the Ivy League. Eric Williams, as was indicated, not only won an island scholarship, but actually came to the Capstone to teach. It was during his tenure at the Capstone that his seminal work, *Capitalism and Slavery*, was published by the University of North Carolina Press in 1944. The book developed from his doctoral dissertation. He had earned the Ph.D. from Oxford in 1938, and C. L. R. James is reported to have been Williams's unofficial dissertation advisor. For a few years, Williams and Cook were fellow faculty members at the Capstone.

There exists a tradition of the confluence at the Capstone of African American and West Indian intellectuals who have been given the best Eurocentric education. It was indicated earlier that the Capstone has been the point of connection and of intellectual fermentation for generations of West Indian scholars. Of late, Howard University recruiters have begun to scour the West Indies in search of young people who have performed well on the university entrance exam, the SAT. The Affirmative Action Program in higher education has had the effect of siphoning off the high-scoring Africans from the United States to the most prestigious white institutions. The depressed economies of the West Indian countries make university education in United States beyond the reach of any but the very wealthy. Thus offers from the Capstone appear to be incredibly generous to the high-scoring prospective university students from the West Indies, or, more precisely, to the parents of these individuals.

So far, then, it has been easy for Howard to attract high numbers of West Indian secondary school graduates who have earned scores of 1300, 1400, and even 1500 in the SAT. The famed island scholarship program has been significantly expanded in Trinidad and Tobago, for instance. However, there are many, many more brilliant students than there are scholarships. Offers from the Capstone help to address the severe imbalance.

It was argued in *Willie Lynch to the World Trade Center* that:

> The graduate programs at the Capstone are peopled by foreign students, many of them West Indians. West Indians are well represented in the ranks of the faculty. The flow of expertise continues along the same lines today as it did from the very beginning of Europe's brutal incursion into the Western Hemisphere. The Capstone would do well, then, to go with the flow. (64)

The basis for the position articulated above is that humanity's earliest historical records were created by Nubians who were the first to develop both writing and a nation state. It is here, then, in the Nile Valley that we find the earliest documented institutions of higher learning, the temple schools. The final chapter of this current book addresses again the matter of education in Kemet.

Africans, who by studying the laws of nature founded those civil and religious systems which still govern the world, declared that their ancestors and teachers lived in the heart of the continent. It is reasonable to speculate that the body of knowledge presented in a work such as Marcel Griaule's *Conversations with Ogotemmêli* would have been developed in institutions of higher learning which would have existed thousands of years before those in Kemet, of which latter we have documented evidence.

In the posthumously published, *Civilization or Barbarism*, Diop declares:

> the "Greek miracle" will begin, as a consequence of the occupation of Egypt by the foreigner, Greek in particular, and therefore of the forced access to the scientific treasures of Egypt, of the plundering of the temple libraries and of the submission of the priests. . . .
>
> The theorem attributed to Thales is illustrated by the figure of problem 53 of the *Rhind Papyrus*, written thirteen hundred years before the birth of Thales. . . .
>
> Herodotus calls Pythagoras a simple plagiarist of the Egyptians: Jamblichus, biographer of Pythagoras, writes that all the theorems of lines (geometry) come from Egypt.
>
> According to Proclus, Thales was the first Greek pupil of the Egyptians and that after his return he introduced science in Greece, particularly geometry. After teaching what he knew to his pupil Pythagoras, he advised him to go to Egypt, where he (Pythagoras) remained for twenty-two years in the temples, in order to learn geometry, astronomy, etc. (cf. Jamblichus, *Life of Pythagoras*).
>
> An Egyptian priest told Diodorus of Sicily that all the so-called discoveries that made Greek scholars famous were things that had been taught to them in Egypt and which they called their own, once they went back to their country. (256-57)

Thomas Jefferson might be excused on the basis of ignorance for his outrageously racist pronouncements in *Notes on the State of Virginia*, for example:

> Comparing them [i.e. Africans] by their faculties of memory, reason, and imagination, it appears to me, that in memory they are equal to the whites; in reason much inferior, as *I think one could scarcely be found capable of tracing and comprehending the investigations of Euclid.* (139 Emphasis added)

That excuse has worn pretty thin these days. Nonetheless, there are still many contemporary academics and makers of public policy who cling tenaciously to the outmoded, preposterous propositions of Jefferson, Willie Lynch, and the like.

Howard University, through a conscientious commitment to the ages-old tradition of African higher education, could reasonably aim at surpassing its status as the Capstone of Negro education. It could actually begin to provide "leadership for America and the global community." West Indian intellectuals must continue to play an important role in this thrust of the Capstone towards its rightful position.

CHAPTER TWO

Self-Affirmation for West Indians in Central America

Don't want nobody to give me nothing.
Just open up the door, and I'll get it myself.
JAMES BROWN

Juana Isidra Dawkins was married to the representative West Indian intellectual on December 23, 1978. She was born at least thirty-nine years ago in the town of Almirante in the province of Bocas del Toro, in the Republic of Panama. Her mother, Mary Dawkins, had carefully chosen the names for this her second child: Isidra, after one of the beautiful baby's aunts, and Juana, because this name, the feminine form of Juan [John], signified strength, creativity, vibrancy, prophetic insight. In accordance with the established administrative procedures in rural Panama at least thirty-nine years ago, the paperwork for registering the birth was sent by mail to the appropriate governmental office in the capital city of the republic.

Some years later, when Mary Dawkins was applying for a passport for her teenage daughter to travel to the United States, she discovered that the administrative apparatus had mistakenly established "Juana" as "Buena." Clearly, some petty provincial functionary, perhaps barely literate, had read "Juana" as "Buena" and so inscribed it in the record. The cost for effecting the correction would have been exorbitant. So Juana retained forever the official name of Buena, but, to her mother and everyone else, she remained "Juana" or simply "Juanita."

Bocas del Toro is the province on Panama's Caribbean coast which borders with the Costa Rican province of Limón. For the Africans who migrated to Central America from the Caribbean islands, the border between Panama and Costa Rica is merely one more of a series of inconveniences to be endured as a consequence of living in a country controlled by others. Hence these Central American Africans of West Indian origin move freely from Limón to Bocas del Toro. Juanita's mother was herself born in Limón, Costa Rica on June 1, 1918 (considerably more than thirty-nine years ago), one of three children (all girls) to Hezikiah Emanuel Dawkins, an African from Jamaica who emigrated to Costa Rica at the end of the nineteenth century as a young man in his late teens.

The African Woman as Leader

Mary Dawkins is one of the most outstanding examples of the triumph of the African over the persistent program of systematic underdevelopment implemented by Europe since the middle of the fifteenth century. The story of migration to Central America by Africans who had taken up residence in the islands of the Caribbean is one of mythical proportions. It is analyzed within a literary studies perspective in *Central American Writers of West Indian Origin: A New Hispanic Literature.* Dawkins, the patriarch, was part of the third wave of migration in the nineteenth century. The first major wave was the expulsion of the people known as the Garifuna in 1797 by the unscrupulous British.

These Garifuna were the product of intermarriage between Africans and the aboriginal peoples of the Caribbean. The two original peoples had merged in the island called Yurumei (alternatively, "Yurumein" or "Yurumain") which the colonial powers renamed St. Vincent. With the draconian insensitivity typical of the colonizing machine, the entire group were simply put on boats and shipped away to Central America.

It is generally believed that this forced migration would have been the second one inflicted on these people. This belief flows from the assumption that the African presence in the Western Hemisphere came about solely as a consequence of the trans-Atlantic slave trade, the greatest crime against humanity. Ivan Van Sertima's work, *They Came Before Columbus,* compellingly challenges these assumptions. It is reasonably certain that the Garifuna group began to evolve prior to 1492. This group would have resulted from the intermingling of African traders and voyagers with the native Arawaks. The Garifuna people currently constitute a significant population group in Belize and Honduras principally, but they are also to be found in Guatemala and Nicaragua.

The wave of migration from the islands to Central America out of which Dawkins the patriarch came was the one which was generated in the 1870s. The nineteenth century was the period during which the Europeans of the original Thirteen Colonies in North America created their American empire. This empire was limited to the confines of the continent of North America. Its juridical foundation was the Treaty of Tordesillas. By then the concept of the "manifest destiny" of European nations to hold sway over the entire Western Hemisphere had been expanded to include more than just the two nations of the Iberian Peninsula. Once the Europeans of the Thirteen Colonies had established their independence from the British Crown, they were permitted to join the inner circle of empire builders. However, it was understood that their empire building would be limited to the North American continent.

The quest for gold was the engine which drove the process of "discovery." And in 1849 the Europeans, who had been granted the right to exploit the immense wealth of the North American continent, found their own pot of gold at the end of the trail. There remained still vast reaches of difficult terrain populated by natives who were slow to acknowledge the absolute rights granted by God to his favored Europeans over the possessions and persons of the aboriginal peoples. The sea route between the Pacific and the Atlantic could be considerably shortened through transshipment by land across the Isthmus of Panama. There was, consequently, urgent need to construct a railroad across this Isthmus for much more efficient transshipment.

Construction of the trans-isthmian railroad was initiated in 1850 under the direction of the British, the pioneers in rail systems. Having been forced to terminate the physical enslavement of Africans in their Caribbean colonies, the British were faced with the growing problem of trying to maintain dominance over a majority population now engaged in the reconstruction of their society in accordance with a tradition of civilized existence which dated back to the beginning of recorded history. With the malevolence and ruthless cunning which characterize the colonizer, the British set about destabilizing the nascent neo-African society. They implemented an intense campaign encouraging Jamaican males to turn from agriculture to labor as semi-skilled workers in railroad construction, the popular industrial sector of the time. The leaders of society promoted the virtues of the high-paying jobs in Panama, seducing thousands of young men to abandon the traditions on which civilization itself was built.

The railroad construction brought a great boom to Panama. It was short-lived, however, for the very year in which the trans-isthmian railroad was completed the Europeans in the North opened their transcontinental railroad. Once they tasted life in Panama, the majority of the Jamaican workers opted to take their chances with the nonagricultural sector. Life on the land had lost its charm. They opted to stay on in Panama.

Around 1870, the Costa Rican government decided to avail itself of the benefits of a rail system. This system would connect the Caribbean port town of Limón to the inland high plateau centers of population. The Spanish colonizers had consistently chosen to locate their administrative centers in the cooler highland regions, eschewing the heat and humidity of the coastal regions. The original railroad project failed. However, two enterprising North American whites created the legendary United Fruit Company making use of the available Jamaican migrant workers.

Many of the Jamaicans who had come to Costa Rica in this 1870 wave refused to hire themselves out to work on the banana plantations, which could not have been very different from the sugar plantations of the Caribbean and Latin America or the cotton plantations of the South. The Jamaicans found the tropical coastal regions of Costa Rica to be very similar to their adopted homeland as well as their true home, Guinea. They, then, immediately took advantage of the opportunity offered. They recreated in Costa Rica the society which their parents and grandparents had begun to construct in Jamaica at the end of the hellish system of physical enslavement.

Word went back to Jamaica that Costa Rica was a land of possibilities. When Dawkins the patriarch arrived in Limón, Costa Rica in his late teens at the end of the nineteenth century, he came not to work as a laborer but as a small farmer, a planter. These Jamaicans brought to Costa Rica a style of agricultural development which had been passed on to them through the many millennia of civilized existence. It is a technique which makes for the most efficient and ecologically sound use of the land. The current government of Costa Rica puts heavy emphasis on ecotourism and uses the now outmoded West Indian small farms as museum pieces, reminders of a glorious past. In Ecuador, in the coastal regions of the province of Esmeraldas, Africans settled and developed the same methods of farming. However, the dominant minority in that country, whites and mestizos, still blinded by white supremacy excoriate the African farming system as wasteful and conducive to the inherent sloth of unlettered savages.

Whereas the Jamaican African style of farming is lauded now with warm fuzzy nostalgia, the real Jamaicans such as Dawkins the patriarch were marginalized by the Costa Rican central government. Indeed, the feeling was mutual, for those old-time Jamaicans were a proud people. They came from the exact same stock as the Honorable Marcus Mosiah Garvey, to whom is credited the adage: "do for self." Efficient development of their holdings of about ten hectares enabled Dawkins and his people to be entirely self-sufficient. To earn the cash they needed to buy the materials they did not produce, they cultivated cocoa.

The Africans from Jamaica knew themselves to have descended from those people who, in the much quoted words of the Frenchman, Count Constantin François de Chassebœuf de Volney, "by studying the laws of nature, discovered those civil and religious systems which still govern the world." Education, what the ancient Kemites termed *sb3yt*, was the foundation of society. Uprooted from their ancestral lands, held in brutal captivity by a vicious European system, the Jamaicans had lost some of the clarity of their ancestors. They now equated their ancestral *sb3yt* with the European academic system built on fundamentally duplicitous dogmas. This was, unfortunately, characteristic of people subjected to the intense programming described in and symbolized by the speech attributed to Willie Lynch. (See "Putting Willie Lynch in Perspective" in *Willie Lynch to the World Trade Center.*)

The liberation from physical enslavement was achieved finally by 1888 in Brazil, the last nation in the Americas to end the vicious system. Nonetheless, the struggle against mental slavery continues. The Haitians, for all the glory they achieved in their military endeavors, never attained liberty from mental slavery. John Jacob Thomas confronted with clarity and courage the assaults on his people by the European academic system. However, he too fell victim to some of the white supremacist programming. He saw Latin and Greek as the "classical" languages, as did Dr. Martin Luther King, Jr., and as does Howard University, the Capstone of Negro education.

Dawkins and his people created an independent educational system. It is not, then, a happenstance that the personality at the center of the most significant act of resistance of the West Indian workers in Panama was, in the words of the West Indian Panamanian poet, Gerardo Maloney:

> Preston Stoute
> Maestro barbadiense y dirigente de la gesta (19)
> [Preston Stoute

Barbadian teacher and leader of the heroic feat]

This couplet constitutes the climactic centerpiece of the long poem, "1920," of Maloney's collection *Juega vivo*.

Teachers from back home hired by Dawkins and his people were, as was Preston Stoute, intellectuals and activists of the caliber of John Jacob Thomas, of George G. M. James, of C. L. R. James. Dawkins and his people refused to speak Spanish, deeming it scornfully a "bird language." They looked down on the culinary skills and the general hygiene of the host population, proudly proclaiming themselves British subjects. In their minds they were as much Englishmen as the whites in the far-off mother country. The basis of their society, of their culture, was their education system and their Church, the Anglican Church. Having lost some of their soul, Dawkins and his people had followed their colonizers into the murky waters of male chauvinism. Thus they tended to exclude their womenfolk from the benefits of education.

They had forgotten the profound lessons of the story recounted by the British Egyptologist, E. A. Wallis Budge, whose work was produced at the turn of the twentieth century. Budge, in his introduction to *The Egyptian Book of the Dead,* designates this account as "The Legend of Ra and Isis" and explains in a footnote:

> The hieratic text of this story was published by Pleyte and Rossi, *Le Papyrus de Turin*, 1869-1876, pll. 31-77, and 131-138; a French translation of it was published by M. Lefébure, who first recognized the true character of the composition. (xci)

Isis is a Greek corruption of the name Auset, hailed by the ancient Africans as the great Mother of God. Ra is the sun god. In some of the doctrines developed by the people of Kemet—and it must be remembered that Kemet existed as a unified nation for at least three thousand years—Ra is the name given to the Supreme Being. Indeed, in the first formulation of the doctrine of the Trinity, Ra was seen as one of the three persons composing the One True God.

The text of the legend begins as follows:

> Now Isis was a woman who possessed words of power; her heart was wearied with the millions of men, and she chose the millions of the gods, but she esteemed more highly the millions of the *khu's*. And she meditated in her heart, saying, "Cannot I by means of the "sacred name of God make myself mistress of the earth and become "a goddess like unto Ra in heaven and upon earth?" (lxxxix-xc)

The stage is clearly set. Auset (Isis) is a powerful woman who decides to make herself the most powerful of beings. She is not content with mere preeminence, she sets out to be the most preeminent of all. To do so, she would have to unseat Ra from his position of ultimate preeminence, and she forms precisely this resolve. Ra, the legend tells, is now an old man who dribbles. Auset (Isis) gets hold of some of this saliva, "kneaded it with earth in her hand, and formed thereof a sacred serpent in the form of a spear" (xc).

The serpent stings Ra, and he becomes gravely ill. He cries out:

> ". . . I came forth to look upon that which I had made, I was passing "through the world which I had created, when lo! something stung "me, but what I know not. Is it fire? Is it water? My heart is on fire, "my flesh quaketh, and trembling hath seized all my limbs. Let "there be brought unto me the children of the gods with healing "words and with lips that know, and with power which reacheth "unto heaven." The children of every god came unto him in tears,

> Isis came with her healing words and with her mouth full of the breath of life, with her enchantments which destroy sickness, and with her words of power which make the dead to live. (xc)

The text vividly portrays Ra's powerful position as the creator. However, he is not here the One True God. The Kemites deemed Ra to be a *ntr*, a term translated as "god" with a lower case "g." The One True God is also a *ntr*. In this context, the term *ntr* would have to be translated as "God" with an upper case "G." The Kemetic term is, then, the exact equivalent of the Yoruba "orisha." Eschu Elegbara also called Papa Legba, to whom reference was made in the introduction of the present book, is one of the most important *ntrw* or "orisha" of the Yoruba.

Auset (Isis) is at this point also a powerful being. She is one of the four children of the sky goddess, Mut, and the earth god, Geb. Her siblings are Wosir, Set, and Nephtys. In the realm of mythology, as in the realm of poetry, the principle of non-contradiction does not apply. "A" can be what in the realm of human logic is "Non-A." So, Auset is also Wosir's faithful consort. She it was who doggedly sought out the scattered parts of her slain consort/brother and gathered them together so that he could regain the physical integrity necessary for resurrection. She it was, in fact, who with the help of Djehuti (Thoth) breathed life back into Wosir, thereby effecting his resurrection. This action is referenced in the words of the text, "and with her words of power which make the dead to live."

It must be pointed out that when Auset made the dead Wosir to live again, it was with the life of a resurrected being and as king of the afterlife. Furthermore, although the legend makes no mention of any sexual congress, it turns out that Auset becomes pregnant. The clear sense of the Kemetic doctrine is that this was a case of parthenogenesis, a further manifestation of Auset's power. Over the many millennia during which the Kemetic theology was developed, Wosir became indistinguishable from his and Auset's son, Heru (whom the Greeks called Horus). In the realm of mythology, then, Auset is sister, wife, and mother to Wosir.

Auset (Isis) drives a hard bargain: if Ra wants to be loosed from the deadly effects of the venom, he will have to reveal to her his secret name. Ra is, naturally, loathe to do so and attempts to pull rank.

> "I have made the heavens and the earth, I have ordered the moun-
> "tains, I have created all that is above them, I have made the water,
> "I have made to come into being the great and wide sea, I have
> "made the 'Bull of his mother,' from whom spring the delights of
> "love. I have made the heavens, I have stretched out the two
> "horizons like a curtain, and I have placed the soul of the gods
> "within them. I am he who, if he openeth his eyes, doth make the
> "light, and, if he closeth them, darkness cometh into being. At his
> "command the Nile riseth, and the gods know not his name. I have
> "made the hours, I have created the days, I bring forward the
> "festivals of the year, I create the Nile-flood. I make the fire of life,
> "and I provide food in the houses. I am Khepera in the morning, I
> "am Ra at noon, and I am Tmu at even." (xc-xci)

Auset (Isis) is not impressed with this recitation of power. She replies with consummate cheekiness: "What thou hast said is not thy name. O tell it unto me, and the poison shall depart" (xci).

There is a remarkable scene in the New Testament which reflects somewhat the one presented in this Kemetic legend. It is the scene of the meeting between Jesus and the Samaritan woman. She is just as cheeky as Auset. She points out to the Son of God that here he is talking about giving her living water and he doesn't even have the wherewithal to obtain just plain old common or garden water. She reminds him that she is the one with the bucket and that He is the one who asked her for a drink, because he clearly had no bucket.

Auset (Isis) prevails:

> Now the poison burned like fire, and it was fiercer than the flame and the furnace, and the majesty of the god said, "I consent that Isis shall search into me, and that my name shall pass from me into her." Then the god hid himself from the gods, and his place in the boat of millions of years was empty. (xci)

Ra's concession cost him his standing among the gods.

The text makes clear that Auset gained power over Ra not for herself but for her son. "And when the time arrived for the heart of Ra to come forth, Isis spake unto her son Horus, saying, 'The god hath bound himself by an oath to deliver up his two eyes' (i.e., the sun and moon)" (xci). The parallels with Mary and Jesus are significant. It must be recalled that it was at the Council of Ephesus in A.D. 431 that the new Way, which came to be called Christianity, promulgated the dogma that Mary was the Mother of God (*Theotókos*). The term "Mother of God" was precisely one of the greatest of the praise names for Auset.

The closing lines of text of the legend proclaim an all-powerful Auset (Isis).

> Thus was the name of the great god taken from him, and Isis, the lady of enchantments, said, "Depart, poison, go forth from Ra. O "eye of Horus, go forth from the god, and shine outside his mouth. "It is I who work, it is I who make to fall down upon the earth the

"vanquished poison; for the name of the great god hath been taken "away from him. May Ra live! and may the poison die, may the "poison die, and may Ra live!" These are the words of Isis, the great goddess, the queen of the gods, who knew Ra by his own name. (xci)

Consistent with the "phallocentric" orientation of so-called Western culture, an attitude of self-confidence in a poet, usually of the popular tradition, has been termed macho boastfulness. And the prime manifestation of this macho boastfulness is the use of the "I." According to this line of reasoning, Auset is employing here macho boastfulness.

Auset, then, is the first womanist. She is employing the tone of supreme confidence that only a woman can use. Her confidence can thus be termed "womanist boastfulness," and it is clearly presented as superior to any kind of macho boastfulness. It is based on demonstrated superiority, not on wishful thinking. The legend reflects a fundamental belief in the preeminence of the mother. This wins out over the patriarchal thrust of what we call Western civilization. Women born in Limón into an imperfectly recreated African society, having been consigned to the inferior role reserved for the female by the colonizer's cultural tradition, could only rescue their preeminence by becoming "manipulative and bossy." In this, they were following the sacred model of the Great Mother.

The Educational System for West Indians

Mary Dawkins could get no more than a third-grade education. However, with the skills which the African woman has demonstrated from time immemorial, she overcame her circumstances. Mary Dawkins' daughter followed the same path of power taken by her mother and by the Great Mother. By the time Juana Isidra came into this world, the central governments in Panama and Costa Rica had set in place structures and campaigns to frustrate the self-determination of their respective West Indian population groups.

The Panamanian government unequivocally resorted to the educational system as its weapon of choice in the unrelenting war on West Indian selfhood. In 1941, the Panamanian president, Arnulfo Arias, took the draconian step of stripping West Indians of their citizenship. At that point in history, most of these so-called "West Indians" had either been born in Panama or had spent most, if not all, of their adult life in Panama.

Since these former British subjects held such a visceral identification with English, the Panamanian oligarchy sought to strip away this linguistic differential factor. They did so by equating the speaking of English with a lack of patriotism. Of course, since Panama was a virtual colony of the United States, the anti-English campaign had to be carefully orchestrated. It was not a campaign against English, but against the speaking of English by Africans. The oligarchy made sure that they developed fluency in the language of their principals, even as the public school system implemented measures to stamp out the speaking of English among Panamanians of African ancestry.

Ironically, the 1948 progressive revolutionary movement in Costa Rica also significantly curtailed the self-determination of the African-ancestored population of Anglophone Caribbean background. The progressive Eurocentric regime claimed that its aim was the unification of the nation, the incorporation of the marginalized group into the body politic. However, they were incorporated not as equals. In fact, despite the progressive liberal leaning of the new regime, decidedly fascist measures were enacted against the ethnolinguistic minority group. For example, they were prohibited from traveling beyond the limits of the Carribean coastal region in which they had opted to settle.

The West Indians, attentive to the lessons of their cultural heritage, had always understood the value of education. They had, in fact, as was pointed out earlier, created an alternative educational system, one of so-called English schools, through which they ensured the perpetuation of their peculiar cultural values and traditions. These schools might be compared to the phenomenon of the Maha Sabha schools created by East Indians in Trinidad and Tobago. Clearly, the English schools were the primary targets of the measures taken by the central governments in Panama and Costa Rica aimed at reducing West Indians to second-class citizenship. Since the West Indians had already become unclear about some of the fundamental principles on which their pristine civilization was founded, it was easy for the Eurocentric ruling class to lead them by their noses back into inferiority. The Central Americans of West Indian origin had become a people who would not stand up for themselves, so they fell into the traps laid by the oligarchy.

Juana Isidra and her peers were simply incorporated into the national education system. Indeed, the tradition of English school held on Saturdays or on evenings did still exist in Juana Isidra's time; and her guardians dutifully enrolled her in one such school. She recounts that not long after she began attending classes at English school, the teacher, who happened to be the local Anglican priest, struck her once with some sort of whip because she missed an answer to one of his questions. That brought an immediate and irrevocable termination of her attendance at English school.

By the end of her elementary school education, the West

Indian intellectual's spouse was sent to Limón to live with her mother's sister and her family. As in Panama, she was exposed to the same educational system as the rest of the population. She reports an incident which is illustrative. Nurtured in an environment with the characteristically African respect for education, the West Indian intellectual's spouse earned good grades. As a consequence of this, she was awarded a little badge in the form of a star. This was a significant mark of honor for the young girl. One day she got into an altercation with one of her mestiza fellow pupils. The teacher assumed that the young African girl was solely to blame and yanked the star from her. This incident is representative of the pervasive racism in Western society. Affirmative action in that school system meant white or pseudo-white privilege.

The West Indian intellectual's wife emigrated to California to begin her high school career. She entered Pasadena High school, and there found herself excluded from the African American cliques. Her African American fellow students were now at least two generations removed from their cultural roots in the South and had lost their respect for education. The new immigrant had not, so she was seen as an outsider. She found her niche among the students who took the process seriously.

Upon graduating from high school, the West Indian intellectual's wife immediately went on to junior college. This was the expected thing to do here in America where the opportunity existed. Then she became the beneficiary of one of the initiatives of the Affirmative Action Program in higher education. She was chosen to attend UCLA, the most prestigious institution in Los Angeles and one of the most respected public universities in the United States.

This particular initiative turned out to be simply a revolving door program which involved bringing in every year a new "crop" of "minorities." The university would be awarded funds on a per capita basis for these "minorities," the vast majority of whom would have failed out by the third quarter, just in time to make room for a new crop. Some survived, and the West Indian intellectual's wife was one of those, inspired by the spirit of Auset, attentive to the example of her own mother, Mary Dawkins, with whom she had been united upon her coming to America. The experience of the West Indian intellectual's spouse is one of the success stories of the Affirmative Action Program developed as part of the Civil Rights legislation

The Limits of the Affirmative Action Program

The voices of so-called "objectivity" from within the ranks of the mainstream Academy have consistently criticized the Negritude movement for overstepping its bounds. Jean-Paul Sartre is the quintessential goodly European intellectual who has been universally accepted as the patron of Negro self-actualization. The glaring contradiction inherent in this seems to have escaped the attention of Academe. So Sartre, the progressive European intellectual of the twentieth century, made Negritude into a respectable literary movement when he wrote the essay, "Orphée Noir," as the introduction to the *Anthologie de la nouvelle poésie nègre et malgache de langue française* [An Anthology of New Black and Madagascan Poetry in French] produced by Léopold Sédar Senghor in 1948. This anthology did for Negritude exactly what Alain Locke's *The New Negro* did for the so-called Harlem Renaissance in 1925.

Sartre's very term Black Orpheus proceeds from the fundamental distortion of historical data, which is white supremacy, dismissing without consideration the very idea of the "The African Origin of Civilization." Of course, Senghor presents himself as the quintessential "Negro" intellectual, for without too much dissembling, he declares Europe to be reason and Africa to be emotion.

Sartre proclaims in his "Orphée Noir":

> En fait, la Négritude apparaît comme le temps faible d'une progression dialectique : l'affirmation théorique et pratique de la suprématie du blanc est la thèse ; la position de la Négritude comme valeur antithétique est le moment de la négativité. Mais ce moment négatif n'a pas de suffisance par lui-même et les noirs qui en usent le savent fort bien ; ils savent qu'il vise à préparer la synthèse ou réalisation de l'humain dans une société sans races. (xli)
> [Indeed, Negritude would be considered the opposite pole in a dialectical progression: the theoretical and practical affirmation of white supremacy is the thesis; Negritude as the antithesis of this is the negative pole. But this negative pole is not sufficient unto itself and Blacks who use it are keenly aware of this; they know that it is focused on preparing the synthesis, the attainment of a truly human, raceless society.]

The Cuban poet, Nicolás Guillén (1902-1989), is championed by mainstream scholars as the representative par excellence of the black voice in Latin American letters. Guillén is one of those "noirs" [Blacks] for whom Sartre in his capacity as great white father speaks. For the Cuban asserted quite clearly that he did have the proper understanding of what's what claimed for him by Sartre. Guillén made it clear in an interview published in Nancy Morejón's *Recopilación de textos sobre Nicolás Guillén* that Negritude was not to be allowed to develop *à outrance* [beyond accepted bounds].

> Con la negritud sucede como con el realismo socialista, del que todo el mundo da una explicación distinta y tal vez todos tienen razón. . . . Era una de las manifestaciones de la lucha de clases. Pero cuando una revolución borra esa lucha y da el poder a la clase obrera sin tener en cuenta el color de la piel, ese concepto de superioridad o de diferenciación racial deja de existir. Hay momentos — momentos históricos — en que la negritud está ligada a los movimientos de liberación nacional; pero es imposible mantenerla como una actitud *à outrance*, porque entonces se convertiría en otro racismo. (44-45)
> [You find the same with Negritude as with socialist realism, everybody explains it in a different way, and they all are perhaps on target. . . . It (Negritude) was one of the manifestations of the class struggle. But when a revolution comes along and erases this struggle and empowers the working class without distinction as to skin color, that concept of racial superiority or differentiation ceases to exist. There are moments—historical moments—in which Negritude is bound up with national liberation movements; you can't take Negritude beyond accepted limits, otherwise it will become another form of racism.]

Negritude, therefore, is to be exactly what the great white father in his omnipotence over Negroes assigned it to be:

> . . . car la Négritude n'est pas un état, elle est pur dépassment d'elle-même, elle est amour. C'est au moment où elle se renonce qu'elle se trouve ; c'est au moment où elle accepte de perdre qu'elle a gagné : à l'homme de couleur et à lui seul il peut être demandé de renoncer à la fierté de sa couleur. (xlii)
> [. . . for Negritude is not a permanent state of being, it is pure self-effacement, it is love. It is when it denies itself that it finds itself; it is when it agrees to lose itself that it triumphs: it is only the colored man and him alone who can be asked to renounce pride in

his color.]

Sartre, like most of the leading existentialist philosophers, was not a Christian. Albert Camus, one of Sartre's most distinguished followers, in his pivotal novel, *La Peste* [The Plague], presented through the words of Tarrou, one of the important characters of the novel, the major problem of modern man as:

> — Justement. Peut-on être un saint sans Dieu, c'est le seul problème concret que je connaisse aujourd'hui. » (204).
> ["Exactly. Can you be a saint if there is no God, that's the sole concrete problem I know of today."]

However, Sartre emasculates Negritude using the language of Christ himself. The Divine Master enjoined on his followers that they deny themselves, take up the cross, and follow him. He specified that he who loses his life will find it and he who finds his life through sin will lose it. White supremacist Christianity has consistently distorted the Master's words to support its unholy system, enjoining on Africans that they deny their African self in order to follow Christ. Sartre analogously calls on Africans to renounce their Africanness in order to find their humanity.

The Affirmative Action Program does, indeed, work best when it is envisaged not as a permanent state of being, but a shot in the arm, in Sartre's words: "pur dépassment d'elle-même." The Welfare Program works best when used also as a temporary measure to redress the inequalities created by white supremacy. The proposed reparations for the monumental injustices of the trans-Atlantic slave trade, the enslavement of Africans, and institutionalized racism which persists even to this very day analogously correspond to lifelines out of the deep pit of despair. If any of these Programs become a permanent way of life, they can then be deemed to have been unsuccessful.

The Affirmative Action Program in education is meant to help those who have been significantly disadvantaged through the racist affirmative action policies on which the United States was founded. Having earned a graduate degree at one of the premiere universities in the nation, the West Indian intellectual's wife moved on to the next phase of life, inspired by the example of her natural mother and of the Great Mother.

Many individuals use the Affirmative Action Program as a permanent crutch. In this respect, they are similar to the infamous "welfare queens," those hapless persons who exist to be on welfare. In Academe, the equivalent of the welfare queen would be the person who, having earned a graduate degree through the Affirmative Action Program, opts to remain in the system as an instructor at the tertiary level. Such individuals in effect subvert the established order in Academe; for, from the very beginning of civilization (in the Nile Valley at the dawn of history), instructors at the tertiary levels have traditionally been bona fide intellectuals.

The master's degree was formerly the entry level requirement for a faculty position. Now it is merely the terminal degree for the fully prepared professional. The doctorate has become the entry level requirement for a faculty position, with the understanding that faculty members are to be bona fide intellectuals. The "welfare queen" approach to education leads individuals to consider the doctorate merely as the ticket to the comfortable life of the university professor, and not as the introduction to a life of study. The West Indian intellectual's wife did not fall into the "welfare queen" trap. Not having a taste for the life of study, she declined the seductive invitation to teach at the college level. She also avoided the temptation of the government job or the mid-level management position in the corporate world. Inspired by her mother's energies, she went into business for herself; she became self-employed.

The most fundamental of all business is trade: you buy something and sell it. However, in the circles of the sophisticated black middle class, it is *infra dignitatem* to engage in trade. The African American under the age of thirty who emerges from college with a graduate degree would avoid like the plague such an activity as peddling cosmetics or soap, or even "self-published" books for that matter. The West Indian intellectual's wife, upon completing the M.A. in Latin American studies from UCLA, became a Mary Kay "consultant." The sophisticated middle-class African Americans enjoying the "security" of their mid-level management jobs looked askance at the young woman with an accent who sold cosmetics and appeared to have a seriously limited wardrobe.

The progression from cosmetics to real estate was a natural one. Even though real estate agents are deemed to be independent contractors, the vast majority are nothing more than salaried workers, and low-paid at that. The West Indian intellectual's wife did for self in the universe of realtors becoming de facto as well as de jure an independent contractor. She is affiliated with Re/Max, and as such she, indeed, works for herself.

The Affirmative Action Program in higher education developed as a result of the Civil Rights movement is a phenomenon peculiar to the United States. Affirmative action as white (or pseudo-white) privilege is the basic building block of Western societies, and this is the only form which exists in Central America. Those of her peers left behind in Panama and Costa Rica when the West Indian intellectual's wife emigrated, had to call upon all of the resources bequeathed to them by their Great Mother. Many are the West Indian Panamanians and Costa Ricans who prevailed over the pseudo-white supremacist status quo, and among these have been women, daughters of the Great Mother, the quintessential womanist.

Scholarship as Struggle in the Central American West Indian Tradition

The West Indian intellectual's first book was *Central American Writers of West Indian Origin: A New Hispanic Literature* (Washington, D.C.: Three Continents Press, 1984). As a doctoral student at UCLA, the West Indian intellectual, Ian Isidore, met his exact namesake from Panama, Juana Isidra. The West Indian intellectual from the very beginning of the course of studies at UCLA had proposed writing as his doctoral dissertation "West Indianness in the Poetry of Nicolás Guillén." This project was ultimately vetoed by his professors in the Department of Spanish and Portuguese. They found the topic too "anthropological"—or that was the euphemism for which they opted. The final version of the dissertation was entitled: "The Creative Dialogue in the Poetry of Nicolás Guillén: Europe and Africa."

Energized, fulfilled by his union with the West Indian daughter of the Great Mother, the West Indian intellectual focused his scholarly attention on his people from Central America. His first book chronicled the triumph of these people in the literary enterprise. Under the unrelenting onslaught of the affirmative action of white and near-white privilege, Central American writers of West Indian origin succeeded in creating a new Hispanic literature. By telling their story, the West Indian intellectual gave legitimacy to their achievement, joining them in their fundamental thrust towards reestablishing their selfhood. The book, furthermore, blazed a new trail in Hispanic as well as Caribbean studies, proclaiming with solid documentation the cultural unity of the Caribbean. This approach to the region is one which has attracted the attention of the relatively new Association of Caribbean States.

The Costa Rican Eulalia Bernard is the only female writer of the four major ones presented in the West Indian intellectual's book. She is of the same lineage as the West Indian intellectual's wife, although the two are separated in years by almost one generation. Bernard is a poet who writes mostly in Spanish. However, her English is fluent, and she is culturally no different from the five million people who inhabit the Anglophone Caribbean.

The other Costa Rican studied in the West Indian intellectual's first book is Quince Duncan. He happened to have been born in 1940 in the capital city, San José, but his home province is Limón. This is the home province of Costa Rica's West Indians. Duncan is himself an educator and is numbered among the most respected writers in his country. His published works are written exclusively in Spanish and are primarily novels and short stories, but he is fluent in English. In this respect the Costa Rican West Indians tend to differ from their Panamanian peers. The reason appears to stem from the difference in intensity of the anti-West Indian educational programs as dispensed by the white/mestizo central administration in the two countries.

Carlos Guillermo Wilson was born in Panama in 1941, the very year in which the white/mestizo strongman, Arnulfo Arias, stripped West Indian Panamanians of their citizenship. Wilson triumphed over white/mestizo privilege in Panama, completing his secondary studies at the prestigious Instituto Nacional. He then emigrated to the United States and obtained the Ph.D. from UCLA. He completed his studies in the U.S. without any help from the Affirmative Action Program in higher education developed as a consequence of the Civil Rights movement. Still, he had to confront and overcome the fundamental affirmative action as white privilege. Wilson is a legitimate West Indian intellectual. He is a full professor of Spanish at San Diego State University and is a successful writer who works in prose as well as verse.

Gerardo Maloney, the youngest of the group, was born in Panama in 1945. He is a poet, essayist, film maker, and professor. As such, he is the quintessential intellectual. Maloney completed his secondary studies in Panama and then went to Mexico to study sociology. He completed postgraduate studies in Ecuador. He is the most Latin American of the group of Central American writers of West Indian origin. Whereas he is fluent in conversational English, he tends to avoid delivering formal lectures in that language.

Reliance on education has taken West Indians from Central America a long way. The only affirmative action they have encountered and continue to encounter is the endemic system of white/mestizo privilege. The West Indian intellectual in one of his more recent books, *Willie Lynch to the World Trade Center: An African American Response to Nine-One-One,* unmasks the core strategy developed by whites for perpetuating their privilege. It is the strategy articulated in a speech attributed to one Willie Lynch.

> There runs a rift, deep and seemingly impassable, between *negros antillanos* and *negros coloniales* in Panama. Upon reviewing the preceding discussion, it is impossible to escape the conclusion that,

in the first instance, this great divide in Panama is a direct consequence of policies entirely consonant with those articulated in the Willie Lynch James River speech. Secondly, it can be reasonably concluded that these policies were created and implemented in order to ensure the efficient functioning of an economic order founded on the globalization of trade. This economic order is fundamentally unjust. It was created by Europeans who unconscionably laid claim to all of the resources, property, and even the very personhood of non-Europeans. (98)

CHAPTER THREE

Self-Affirmation in the Anglophone Caribbean

Emancipate yourselves from mental slavery.
None but ourselves can free our minds.
BOB MARLEY

Africans from the West Indies fell hook, line, and sinker for the elaborate British colonial plan to promote white supremacy through education. As was pointed out in the preceding chapter, the West Indians who settled in Panama and Costa Rica during the latter half of the nineteenth century accepted with equal fervor the cultural self-annihilation effected by the British educational system. In the British colonies, the education system was designed to sift young people, relentlessly separating the top one or two percent from the teeming masses.

The Formation Process

In 1954, only 150 children below the age of eleven won an Exhibition scholarship, that is, free tuition at one of the handful of elitist secondary schools in the colony of Trinidad and Tobago. When these young people were ready to sit for the O-level General Certificate of Education, house scholarships (recognition and a bursary for purchasing books) were given only to the top fifty. The advanced level (A-level) examinations were normally taken two years after the O-level. Every year, five favored young people were given "Island scholarships." This was a complete package, tuition, books, subsistence, clothing, travel, to complete a course of study at a university in the North. In chapter 1, reference was made to V. S. Naipaul's stinging commentary on the scholarship winner.

The West Indian intellectual featured in this book won an Exhibition scholarship in 1954 and a house scholarship in 1959. When he returned to school after gaining with fairly decent grades the A-level certificate in 1961, everyone thought that he had been selected to try for an island scholarship. This was not the case, however, for he had decided to study for the priesthood, and the priests who ran the secondary school he attended deemed it prudent that he not enter the work force prior to leaving for Ireland. It was customary for those bright young people who did not earn the highest marks in their group of studies—there were four: languages, sciences, mathematics, and modern studies—to work for a year or two to save the required funds for travel to the North and for the first year of university studies.

The secondary school, called a college, which the West Indian intellectual attended had opened on Emancipation Day (August 1), 1863, with fourteen pupils—of whom eight were boarders and six day-pupils. It had been founded by missionary priests of the Irish province of the Congregation of the Holy Ghost. This order had itself been founded by a French Jew who converted to Catholicism, Fr. Francis Libermann. His burning ambition was the evangelization of Africans. It is no mere coincidence that St. Mary's College and Howard University would have been established within a few years of each other. The missions of both institutions were exactly the same, the formation of a tiny minority of "Negroes," who would be thoroughly indoctrinated into the ways of Western civilization.

Since the state religion of Great Britain is Anglicanism, the colonial educational system was overtly Protestant. However, the majority of the local elite in Trinidad and Tobago were French Creoles, who were Catholic. It is for this reason that the Irish priests of the Congregation were permitted to establish their college. Africans constituted the vast majority of the population in the West Indian colonies. It would not have been cost effective at that point to set up a segregated educational system of the type created by the federal government of the United States right after the Civil War. In fact, since the aim of education was the inculcation of the doctrine of white supremacy, it proved advantageous to the colonial authorities to have their sons (and later on daughters) educated side by side with the anointed natives.

White privilege/entitlement was affirmed, then, principally through the systematic indoctrination process called education. This occurred wherever Europeans held sway. Affirmative action in the educational system devised by the British colonial authorities meant that whites were guaranteed a place in the colleges without any regard to their intellectual capacities. They were promoted without any regard to their merit. It served the interest of the British to allow a few anointed "Negroes" to enter the hallowed halls of the white supremacists academic tradition. It was on this same basis that Will Mercer Cook, for example, attended Amherst College and Brown University. It was also on this basis that the great Negro scholars in the United States went to Harvard and subsequently came to teach at Howard.

From their very inception, the colleges in colonial Trinidad and Tobago admitted anointed Africans. Eventually, this population became the majority one. However, the white students never ceased to be privileged, the beneficiaries of that fundamental affirmative action which has been the bedrock of Western civilization. They did not have to compete with the general pool, a place was guaranteed for them. They were the elite, the whole world revolved around them. The West Indian intellectual's father, who was born in 1917, attended St. Mary's College. By his time, the student population was as much African as European. The senior West Indian intellectual became an attorney, one of the privileged group of natives trained to replace the colonial masters. This training, nevertheless, had as its goal the radical acculturation of the chosen few among the Africans, converting them into Afro-Saxons.

The situation in the West Indian intellectual's time was not essentially different from that which obtained in his father's time or in the time of the first generation of students to attend the college. The white boys had a place reserved for them at the very pinnacle of society through affirmative action. They did not have to study. They were known to be the cream, therefore rich and thick. The non-whites could only make it by the sweat of their brow. They were selected to be the leaven to the dominated masses, but they could only maintain their positions the old-fashioned way, by hard work.

The anointed Africans emerged at the top of the heap through a fiercely competitive process. Although the selection system was based purely on merit, the children of the lumpen proletariat were at a distinct disadvantage, not having even the barest resources necessary for serious involvement in the scholastic life. Only the very brightest and disciplined made it to the highest ranks of the colonial education system, so the competitiveness of the top universities of the North did not faze these young people. Furthermore, having worked for a year or two or more subsequent to completing the A-level, these were very mature young people compared to their European classmates.

The West Indian intellectual went directly from the secondary school to the seminary. The first year of formation is the novitiate, a year of prayer and reflection. This was followed by two years dedicated to the study of philosophy of the school of St. Thomas Aquinas. By the time the young West Indian intellectual entered University College Dublin, he was three years older than his classmates and decidedly more intellectually mature. It was not surprising, then, that he would be one of the top three students in his class in first year economics. He thus qualified to take an honors degree in that subject. Although he wanted to combine economics with Spanish, University College Dublin did not offer the possibility of such a combination. It would have to be economics and politics or French and Spanish.

The course of undergraduate studies in the British system (and the Irish as well) is three years. Students could take either a general or an honors degree. All students did four subjects in the first year, the general degree students narrowed down to three and the honors students to two for the second and third year. Consistent with the weeding-out process at the root of the system, only the students who scored high marks in their first year were allowed to pursue honors degree course in that subject.

The language programs focused precisely on language. Thus the most important of the four papers of the final comprehensive exam was the one which tested the student's ability to write elegantly in the target language. A student attempting an honors degree in French and Spanish would thus have to demonstrate a capacity to write elegant prose in French and Spanish in order to be awarded the degree.

Elegance is a function ultimately of personal preference, so that the students who scored the highest marks in the fundamental papers of the exams were those whose sensibilities were in harmony with the sensibilities of the professors. For a West Indian in Ireland or England, the establishment of this harmony was a tall order. It was, however, a hurdle which every student in the colonial education system had been trained to negotiate; for, in those days, the comprehensive examinations at the ordinary and advanced level of secondary school were prepared and marked in the mother country.

The kind of proficiency in French and Spanish acquired by a student who earned an honors degree from a British or Irish university surpasses that of most students who have earned doctorates in French or Spanish from a university in the United States. It is inconceivable then that a scholar with a B.A. honors in Spanish from, say, University College Dublin, who had to make a presentation in the target language, would first write it in English and then translate it with the help of a dictionary (and perhaps some native speakers) into Spanish. There is at least one highly regarded full professor of Spanish who earned his degree from a very reputable university in the United States who writes first in English the speeches he is charged with delivering in Spanish.

Scholars who have earned legitimate doctorates from reputable departments of French or Spanish in the United States would compare, then, poorly with their peers who received their basic formation in the British/Irish system. To make matters even worse, there has crept into the HBCUs the pernicious custom of appointing as professors of French and Spanish persons who have not earned doctorates in French or Spanish. There are, clearly, exceptions to every rule. And it is possible for a scholar who has earned a doctorate in, for example, foreign language education or applied linguistics to perform efficiently as a professor of French or Spanish. However, each case has to be assessed on its own merits. It does become problematic when a specific department routinely appoints as professors of French or Spanish individuals who have not earned doctorates from reputable departments of French or Spanish.

With the rigorous preparation in Spanish, the West Indian intellectual excelled at the Universidad Nacional Autónoma de México (UNAM) [National Autonomous University of Mexico City]. He went to this institution to pursue studies towards the master's degree in Spanish language and Spanish American literature. The brochures advertised that the degree could be earned in eighteen months. This period comprised three semesters (two regular and one summer session) of course work followed by at least six months spent in developing the thesis.

The course work was not difficult for the West Indian scholar. However, the course in linguistics did present an initial challenge. Indeed, the instructor, a white American, advised the young West Indian scholar to take a preparatory (remedial) class before attempting the first of the two required courses. This would have set back the young West Indian's program, so he opted to take the bull by the horns. Within a few weeks, it became obvious that the young West Indian was the most promising student in that course.

In one calendar year, the young West Indian completed all of the required course work. During the registration process at the beginning of his third regular semester, he indicated to the supervising official that he planned to devote himself entirely to the completion of his thesis and expected to graduate at the end of that semester. The somewhat bemused official replied: "*O, la tesis! Eso es cosa de años*" [Oh, the thesis! Well that takes years to complete]. That incident took place in late January. In August of that very year, the young West Indian defended his thesis, earning a commendation for his work.

The thesis was entitled: "La desesperanza y el humor: el testimonio de Juan José Arreola" [Despair and Humor: The Testimony of Juan José Arreola]. Arreola was at that time one of Mexico's most celebrated writers. He lived in Guadalajara, but happened to be visiting the capital when the young West Indian was ready to defend. Urged on by one of his professors, the young West Indian sought out Arreola, presented him with a bound copy of the thesis, and invited him to attend the forthcoming defense. The celebrated author accepted the thesis and promised to look it over that night, asking the young West Indian to return the next day for the response to his invitation. The next day, the young West Indian was greeted by an enthusiastic Arreola, who said that he had read half of the one-hundred-plus-page thesis, that he found it impossible to put down, and that he would be honored to attend the defense.

After completing the M.A. in Mexico, the young West Indian returned to his native land to teach Spanish, French, and history at the secondary school level. He had gained his first experience as an instructor during the second and third semester he spent at UNAM. In exchange for remission of half of his tuition, he had taught English as a second language. The young West Indian realized that Academe had evolved to the point at which the Ph.D. was the absolute entry level requirement for a faculty position. He applied to four universities to pursue the doctorate in Spanish: Columbia University, the University of Toronto, the University of California Irvine, and the University of California, Los Angeles (UCLA). The latter institution made him the best offer, a three-year teaching fellowship.

The Department of Spanish and Portuguese at UCLA may have taken into consideration the race of the young West Indian when it made him the offer. It was made in the spring of 1971, a period of Civil Rights ferment. However, the young West Indian discovered that he was the most qualified of that year's group of graduate teaching assistants. He had been highly recommended by his professors at UNAM. The Department of Spanish and Portuguese knew that they had found an outstanding scholar. Indeed, the young West Indian proved them right. He completed the required course work in the minimum time. There is just one grade earned by the young West Indian intellectual at UCLA that was not an "A." This was a "B" he was given—as the professor explained—simply because he had missed one session, and that was in order to attend an interview for a summer job. He had obtained permission from the professor to be absent from the class. But, as the saying goes: "them's the breaks."

The relationship between the teacher and student is the foundation of all education. The ancient Africans from Kemet, who created the first known institutions of higher learning, based their educational system on this foundation. Thus the earliest Greek philosophers, including Socrates, Plato, and Aristotle went to Kemet to sit at the feet of learned Africans. The senior scholar who served as the mentor par excellence to the West Indian intellectual during his years at UCLA was Donald Fogelquist. When the young West Indian, fresh from a year's stint as a secondary school teacher in Trinidad and Tobago, entered UCLA, Fogelquist was chair of the Department of Spanish and Portuguese.

Fogelquist was a gentleman and a scholar. He was the kindly elder man who welcomed the new graduate student and sought to ensure that all would go well with him both in his own studies and in his duties as a graduate teaching assistant. Since Fogelquist was a specialist in twentieth century Spanish American poetry, the West Indian intellectual chose him to serve as his principal dissertation advisor.

Self-Affirmation v Mis-education

In 1933, Carter G. Woodson (1875-1950) published his groundbreaking work, *The Mis-education of the Negro*. The book was essentially self-published, for it was a major step forward in the African American's advance to self-determination. Woodson indicts the educational system which created the HBCUs as basically a process of indoctrination in white supremacist values. The mythical Willie Lynch was a member of the British colonial elite from the West Indies. He was kith and kin to the founding fathers of the United States. The system which created the HBCUs is fashioned, then, after the British one and is designed to produce O.B.Es, that is Obedient Boys of the Empire. These products of the colonial process of indoctrination have been brilliantly dubbed, Afro-Saxons. They are "Negroes" who hate themselves, who have turned their backs on their Africanness.

When the West Indian intellectual emerged in 1975 from his long period of preparation with a doctor of philosophy in Hispanic languages and literatures from UCLA, he was well on his way to self-realization, to emancipating himself from mental slavery. The first step had been taken in response to commentaries by a history teacher at St. Mary's College in 1956. This teacher was John Donaldson, who was at that time a young man preparing to go away to study.

Another decisive step was taken as a consequence of the West

Indian intellectual's relationship with his future spouse, who was at that time an undergraduate student at UCLA. The young woman mentioned casually to the doctoral candidate in Spanish that compelling evidence existed that Africans had exerted significant influence on the development of the earliest civilizations in the Western Hemisphere. With the arrogance bred of mis-education, the West Indian intellectual instinctively dismissed his girlfriend's words as mere nonsense.

The ancient Africans from Kemet, the people who invented civilization, declared (as was reported on page 15) that: "Beautiful speech is more hidden than gemstones, yet it is found with servant-women at the millstones." Fortunately, the West Indian intellectual had not been totally ruined by his long period of mis-education. Indeed, with much reluctance, he finally acknowledged that his girlfriend, an undergraduate student, had information which was paradigm-shifting, and in the area of studies in which he was about to be certified by the Academy as a doctor of philosophy. The West Indian intellectual's future spouse gave him then the final push towards full self-determination.

Once he knew which direction to take, the West Indian intellectual found the scholarly vehicles to take him towards his destination. He had learned from the Academy the ways of scholarship, and these he applied to the fascinating body of works he was discovering. The first was John G. Jackson, *Introduction to African Civilization* (Secaucus, New Jersey: Citadel Press, 1970). John Henrik Clarke wrote the introduction to the 1976 edition of the book, which was the one purchased by the West Indian intellectual. Neither Clarke nor Jackson were deemed by the Eurocentric Academy to be preeminent scholars. And, naturally, Jackson's book was not published by a university press. The following excerpt from Clarke's introduction appears on the back cover of the 1976 paperback edition:

> "The picture we get today of Africa in past ages from the history taught in our schools is that Africans were savages and that, although Europeans invaded their lands and made slaves of them, they were in a way conferring a great favor on them, since they brought to them the blessings of Christian civilization," writes John G. Jackson.
>
> With brilliantly objective scholarship, Jackson obliterates that picture in this book, and presents a picture of a human heritage infinitely more rich, colorful, and varied than is generally understood. The book challenges all the standard approaches to African history and will, no doubt, disturb a large number of overnight "authorities" on Africa who will discover that they do not really know the depth of African history and the role that Africans played in creating early human societies.

Far from rushing to embrace Jackson's liberating scholarship, the leadership of the HBCUs generally sought to distance itself from Jackson, and from Clarke as well. Leslie B. Rout, Jr., an African American, had earned the supreme recognition of the mainstream Academy. His book on *The African Experience in Spanish America: 1502 to the Present Day* was published by Cambridge University Press in 1976. This is the same Cambridge which had, early in the eighteenth century, awarded Francis Williams his degree in mathematics and Latin. The West Indian intellectual once wrote to Rout asking about his failure to acknowledge the African roots of Hispanic civilization. In his response Rout impugned Clarke's scholarly credentials and referred the West Indian intellectual to a certain Joseph Harris, an African American who was at the time chair of the Howard University Department of History.

The second work which moved the West Indian intellectual to total emancipation from mental slavery was Chancellor Williams' *The Destruction of Black Civilization: Great Issues of a Race from 4500 B.C. to 2000 A.D.* (Chicago: Third World Press, 1976). In 1976, Third World Press occupied more or less the same position as is currently occupied by Original World Press. Imamu Amiri Baraka said of Williams' work: "This book should be the basis for all so-called Black Studies programs. This is the basic text, necessary for Afrikan mental development in the last part of the 20th century" (Back cover).

Bob Marley lamented in his piece "Redemption Song," "How long will they kill our prophets while we stand one side and watch?" Jackson and Williams were indeed prophets. They died natural deaths at a respectable old age. However, they died in relative poverty and neglect. Africans as a people did indeed stand aside and watch as these two great prophets withered away and died.

Self-Affirmation at the Capstone

Although the West Indian intellectual had every intention of returning home right after completing the doctorate, circumstances dictated another course of action. He took a position as assistant professor of Spanish at the University of Arkansas, Fayetteville. When, however, after only one year, he got the chance to go to the Capstone, he seized the opportunity. It was a dream come true to be at the Capstone, to walk in the shadow of the great African centered scholars, some of whom were West Indian and some of whom were African American. He could read exactly what he wanted. He could continue in the tradition of Jackson, of Clarke, of Chancellor Williams, of Cook. He got to know the legendary Dr. Ben (Yosef ben-Jochannan) and Sterling Brown. He was a colleague of Stephen Henderson.

One of the West Indian intellectual's colleagues in the Department of Romance Languages at the Capstone was Stanley A. Cyrus, who was another kind of West Indian intellectual. Cyrus had pursued all of his studies at Howard, going up to the M.A. in Spanish and then switching to history for the Ph.D. It was not until 1978, one year after the West Indian intellectual came to the Capstone, that a doctoral program was initiated in Romance Languages. Cyrus was an activist intellectual in the tradition of Walter Rodney.

Cyrus, then, was the perfect complement to the West Indian intellectual. As an activist intellectual, Cyrus had established strong ties with the Afro-Hispanic literary world. He had also acquired some experience in journalism. The two West Indian intellectuals teamed up to create the Afro-Hispanic Institute and the *Afro-Hispanic Review.* Cyrus was the president of the former and editor of the latter. The West Indian intellectual was vice president of the Institute and managing editor of the *Review*. An account of the first five years (1982-87) is given in Ian Isidore Smart, "The *Afro-Hispanic Review* ," in *Philosophy and Literature in Latin America*. The central administration at the Capstone manifested at best indifference and at worst hostility to the Institute and *Review*. It is this author's considered opinion that this attitude flowed from an endemic African American chauvinism, the spirit inculcated by the Willie Lynch policy.

Cyrus was recognized throughout Latin America for his knowledge of and experience in the field of Afro-Hispanic literature and culture. Unable to pursue a Ph.D. in Spanish at the

Capstone, his beloved alma mater, Cyrus did the next best thing, a doctorate in Latin American history, writing his dissertation on the Concha uprising in Ecuador as it was treated in the historical novels. Thereby Cyrus became an expert on the works of the Ecuadorian Nelson Estupiñan Bass (1912-2002), one of the most important of Latin America's black writers.

Cyrus was firmly convinced that the Vice President for Academic Affairs, the chief academic officer at the Capstone, had mounted a campaign to force him out of Howard on the grounds that he was not qualified to be an assistant professor of Spanish, not having the doctorate in Spanish. It made no difference that he was regarded as one of the preeminent scholars in the field of Afro-Hispanic literature, that he had written one of the first books in that field, an anthology entitled, *El cuento negrista sudamericana* [The Black Short Story from South America], that he was the driving force behind the Afro-Hispanic Institute and the *Afro-Hispanic Review*.

Cyrus' book was published in Ecuador in 1973 by the Casa de la Cultura Ecuatoriana. The enemies of African self-affirmation could not seek to discredit the book as "self-published." Clearly their representatives at the Capstone, who are just as unrelentingly opposed to authentic African self-affirmation, did not even consider reading Cyrus' work. It is written in Spanish, the same language in which they deemed him to be not sufficiently proficient. It will be indicated later that these Blacks, who had been anointed by Whites to positions of leadership in Negro education, have elevated to the rank of full professor of Spanish an African American who does not hold the Ph.D. in Spanish.

The keepers of culture in Ecuador considered Cyrus to have running through his veins "una buena cuota de sangre hispánica" [a fair share of Hispanic blood]. The scholar who reviewed Cyrus' manuscript and prepared the text for the flap of the book commends him for not being one of those foreign professors who are armchair scholars. The reviewer declares:

> El ha palpado directamente el proceso de las literaturas de nuestros pueblos, en sus continuos viajes y en el contacto directo con los escritores hispanoamericanos.
> [He (Cyrus) has had hands-on experience with the literary expressions emanating from our communities, through his ceaseless travels and through his direct contact with Latin American writers.]

This is the man whom the gatekeepers at the Capstone deemed to be unqualified for the post of assistant professor of Spanish.

The *Afro-Hispanic Review*

The creation of the Institute and the *Review* represented the realization of the Marcus Garvey principle, do for self. They were intended to provide the ultimate authority for the new scholarly discipline, Afro-Hispanic Studies. Thus the Functions of the *Review* were very clearly stated in the front matter of each issue:

> The Foreign Languages and Latin American Studies curricula of many academic institutions in the Americas do not reflect the richness of Afro-Hispanic culture, the considerable body of Afro-Hispanic literature, nor the diverse contributions of Spanish-speaking Blacks to the creation and development of the nations of Latin America and elsewhere. Neither does the study of history in

the region specifically reflect the significant impact of the African presence over the centuries. *Afro-Hispanic Review* was founded in an effort to correct such omissions.

Neither of the two principal founders would have succeeded in this doing-for-self enterprise without the help of Donna Allen, an extraordinary scholar activist. Allen was the creator and the moving force behind the Women's Institute for Freedom of the Press. She was an experienced small press publisher and journal editor. She was a woman of indomitable energy, who always got the job done. She taught the two West Indian intellectuals everything they needed to know about the world of publishing.

Henry J. Richards is listed in the *Review* as simply one of the associate editors. He was, however, the de facto senior editor. Richards is an African who was born in Trinidad and Tobago. He completed his primary and secondary studies under the elitist British colonial educational system. He traveled to the United States to undertake his tertiary studies and received a Ph.D. in Spanish from the University of Minnesota in the 1964, in the period when the only affirmative action was white male privilege. Richards is a scholar in the true sense of the word, and, with his significant input, the new journal succeeded in maintaining the highest editorial standards.

One of the principal objectives of the founders of the *Review* was to afford African-centered scholars an outlet for their publications. Although there was not a flow of manuscripts from black scholars, the founders managed to provide some of their colleagues at the Capstone with the opportunity of having their articles and reviews published. Among the colleagues who took advantage of the opportunity to get published were: Karen Wallace, professor of French, Carrie Cowherd, professor of Graeco-Roman Studies, and

James Davis, professor of Spanish. All three colleagues are African Americans and have been appointed at one time or another to serve as administrators at the Capstone.

It is worthy of note also that the same Howard University official who, in Cyrus's view, was responsible for forcing him out was the one under whose watch an individual of dubious qualifications was appointed to chair the Department of Romance Languages. This individual was an African American faculty member who had not been a candidate for the position, who had had a less than inspiring career as a university administrator.

Furthermore, that man appointed/anointed to lead the Department was called a full professor of French but did not have the doctorate in French. Indeed, his contribution to the field of French and Francophone studies pales in comparison to Cyrus's to his field. It is not the custom in Academe for faculty members to be promoted to the rank of full professor in a field without demonstrated significant contributions to the field. And certainly it is not normal for a person to be appointed assistant professor of French or Spanish without a Ph.D. in French or Spanish respectively. It can be said, then, that this individual had bestowed upon him a benefit which he had not merited and reasonably concluded that this individual was the beneficiary of the Affirmative Action Program in higher education.

According to the established norms, the Vice President for Academic Affairs acted correctly in removing Cyrus from the position. There are those who believe that the Affirmative Action Program in higher education permits and even encourages the suspension of established norms. That full professor of French whose doctoral degree is in foreign language education still serves in the current Department of Modern Languages and Literatures at the Capstone. Recently, the anomaly was introduced into the

Spanish section when another faculty member, also an African American male, with a doctorate in foreign language education was promoted to full professor of Spanish. And to compound the issue, this individual has been repeatedly appointed by the central administration to serve as chair of the Department. This second faculty member, analogous to the first, is not noted for his contribution to Hispanic studies.

Self-Publishing as Self-Affirmation

The bonds which unite Juan Isidro and Juana Isidra are as deep as they are broad, and they symbolize an equally profound relationship between the two groups of West Indians. When the Panamanian Carlos Guillermo Wilson published his first book, *Cuentos del Negro Cubena,* in 1977, it was to his West Indian brother from Trinidad and Tobago and former UCLA classmate that he turned to translate the work into English. Wilson, following the Garvey mandate, had "done for self" in producing this book, for it would be considered self-published.

In 1979, the West Indian intellectual approached Donald Herdeck, a professor of French at Georgetown University who owned Three Continents Press, in an attempt to have the English version published. Herdeck, however, determined that the book would not be marketable, for its disturbing content was not redeemed by any pornographic elements. The West Indian intellectual gained a better understanding of how the publishing world works, and he determined to apply the lesson learned to his own creative writing.

The market is driven not by the intrinsic value of the work but by its acceptability to readers. The disturbing non-pornographic images of Cubena's narrative would not go over well even with the most progressive readers. Herdeck, however, judged that a literary study of the Central American writers of West Indian origin would appeal to the progressive readership which was targeted by small presses such as Three Continents. Such a study would not be of interest to a university press. For university presses must operate well within the limits of the prevailing paradigm. Herdeck therefore immediately offered the West Indian intellectual a contract to write *Central American Writers of West Indian Origin*.

Almost five years elapsed between the date the contract was first signed and the date of publication, 1984. By this time, the West Indian intellectual had himself become a player in the world of publishing. He and Herdeck were, then, *par cum pare*. His self-confidence was boosted by this circumstance, so that when the opportunity presented itself to publish the translation of Cubena's short stories—on which he had been working for a decade—through the Afro-Hispanic Institute, he seized it.

Disingenuous Eurocentric detractors might deem the publishing of *Short Stories by Cubena* to be an act of self-publishing by a vanity press. They could only reach such a conclusion by ignoring the fact that the work resulted from ten years of painstaking labor and consultations not only with Wilson but with other colleagues. Luck is defined as the confluence of preparation and opportunity. The publishing of *Short Stories by Cubena* in 1987 through the Afro-Hispanic Institute Press then qualifies as a lucky break, for the West Indian intellectual and for Afrocentrism. It was above all an act of self-determination.

It was also a lucky break for the West Indian intellectual and for Afrocentrism that his book, *Nicolás Guillén, Popular Poet of the Caribbean*, was published by the University of Missouri Press in 1990. Normally, works presenting controversial theses are not published by university presses. It was just over a decade earlier, during the waning period of the Civil Rights movement, that the West Indian intellectual's professors at UCLA insisted that he tone down the Afrocentrism of his original dissertation, "West Indianness in the Poetry of Nicolás Guillén." It turned out that when the West Indian intellectual first submitted his manuscript to the University of Missouri Press, the leadership at that institution was female and correspondingly progressive.

One of the books which had helped to point the West Indian intellectual on his way to emancipation from mental slavery was Will Mercer Cook's edition and translation of Cheikh Anta Diop. This work, entitled, *The African Origin of Civilization: Myth or Reality* was published by a commercial press in 1976. Since the ancient Egyptians were the first human beings to develop civilization, it is important that Afrocentric scholars study Egypt. The basic tool for this study is a thorough knowledge of the hieroglyphs. Without this tool, the African scholar would be completely at the mercy of Eurocentric Egyptologists. The need for self-determination mandated that the West Indian scholar acquire a solid knowledge of the language and culture of his Egyptian ancestors.

The Capstone, in 1993, hired a University of Chicago trained white female to teach Egyptology. She appeared not to be fazed by the incongruity of a Eurocentric scholar being the vehicle by which Afrocentric students would be introduced to their cherished heritage at the Capstone. On the Smart Talk page of his web site, www.iansmart.com, the West Indian intellectual reports on a manifestation of the incongruity. He tells how the white female Egyptologist taught, in her first semester course on hieroglyphs, that the term black had for the ancient Egyptians the very same negative connotations it carries in the Eurocentric universe. She must have known that this was absolutely not the case, that, in fact, the term black [*km*] also meant complete or perfect.

The fundamental contradiction of the white female Egyptologist's position at the Capstone was made manifest in several ways. In her zeal to conform to the ideological excesses of Eurocentric Egyptology, she at times crossed the line between faith and science. For example, she confidently asserted that the Egyptian theories of creation were fundamentally different from the accounts presented by Christians. She claimed that the Egyptians held that the Uncaused Cause emerged from the *Nun*, which was not mere emptiness but rather pure potency. The Christian accounts, according to her, all held that the original chaos was pure emptiness; it was nothing, *nihil*, no thing. She, then, posits a major distinction between pure potency and nothing. She appears to be reasoning from a basis of dogma rather than with the open mind of the true philosopher.

The white female Egyptologist once emphatically affirmed that the Christian term "Amen" could not possibly have derived from the Egyptian "Amon." She based her finding on the difference between the vowel "e" and the vowel "o." Even a scholar trained in archeology should have sensed the absurdity of such reasoning. In Middle Egyptian, the primary language of the hieroglyphs, only the consonants are written. Contemporary Egyptologists routinely supply the neutral vowel sound known as the *schwa* between consonants to facilitate pronunciation. In such an environment, the vowel is absolutely fluid.

One of the features of the syntax of Middle Egyptian is the so-called "non-verbal sentence." This feature is described by experts in Creoles as the suppression of the copula, a phenomenon which is typical of African languages. According to this rule, there is no need to link a predicate adjective to its subject with the verb "to be." Egypt is part of Africa. It follows then that Middle Egyptian is an African language. It is perfectly natural that Middle Egyptian would share syntactic features with other African languages and with the Creole languages, which all have the selfsame African syntax. The white female Egyptologist was extremely uneasy with any attempt to compare *her* Middle Egyptian to *our* Creoles.

The information brochure prepared to give exposure to Original World Press states:

> A small press based in Port-of-Spain, Trinidad, OWP was founded in 1994 on the principle of "do for self." It seeks to provide a vehicle for those voices from the original world that have traditionally been excluded from the major publishing enterprises of the north.

Founding a press is one of the most complete ways for an intellectual to do for self, to respond to the injunction: liberate yourself from mental slavery. The West Indian intellectual had gone through a training process. He had been involved in publishing for more than a decade when he founded Original World Press. And the founding of this entity was the culmination of a process which had begun with the first glimmer of consciousness awakened by his form two history teacher. It was a process inspired by the dictates and example of Marcus Garvey and by several generations of West Indian intellectual activists. The example of the Afrocentric scholars who were the mentors of Molefi Kete Asante and the current exponents of Afrocentrism also served to bring the West Indian intellectual to the point of creating Original World Press.

Language and the educational system are the primary weapons used to impose and maintain the regime of mental slavery. The term, Third World, connotes third class and serves to normalize the notion of white supremacy, for the subconscious mind necessarily juxtaposes Third World to First World, that is, third class to first class. The North constitutes the First World, the South is the Third World; the North is populated by first-class people, the South correspondingly, by third-class people.

The West Indian intellectual coined the expression Original World as an act of resistance to mental slavery. If a comparison is to be made between the North and the South, it should be articulated in a manner which empowers rather than disparages the people from the South, the vast majority of mankind, the original people. For if, indeed, as the data compellingly argue, Africa is the cradle of human civilization, then that area of the globe to which Africa belongs should legitimately be labeled the Original World.

Moreover, Europeans constitute a minority of the world's population, and a small minority at that. However, Africans in the United States have been hoodwinked into seeing themselves as "minorities." African Americans who would seethe with indignation at being referred to as "boys" or "girls" proudly proclaim themselves "minorities." They fail to see the very glaring association between "minor" and "minority." They fail to see that the terms "boy" and "girl" are absolutely synonymous with "minor." It is not far-fetched to conclude that those who coined the term minority had uppermost in their mind the identification of African Americans as "boys" and "girls."

Léopold Sédar Senghor, the Senegalese intellectual who was one of the founders of the Négritude movement, was proud to proclaim that Europe is intelligence, Africa is emotion. The West Indian intellectual understood that self-affirming action needed to be taken to reverse the self-hatred inculcated by the Eurocentric Academy. The naming of his commercial publishing enterprise Original World Press was precisely the kind of self-determining action needed to counteract the centuries of affirmative action as white male privilege/entitlement. His affirmative action flowed from self-determination.

In the early 1990s, the West Indian intellectual finally responded to the call to engage in creative writing. He saw the writer as the agent of the Yoruba orisha, Eschu Elegbara, more familiarly known as Papa Legba. Papa Legba is himself a manifestation of the Egyptian *ntr* Djehuti (whom the Greeks called Thoth), who is known in Graeco-Roman antiquity as Hermes. The griot is the agent par excellence of Legba or Djehuti or Hermes. In the immediate cultural heritage of the West Indian intellectual it is the kaisonian who functions as the griot. Griots are masters of the art of verbal war, and these verbal confrontations are central to the cultural traditions of African peoples throughout the globe. In contemporary African American culture these verbal face-offs are called "free style."

In the "free style" contests between kaisonians, the chorus most frequently ends with the expression "*sans humanité*," [no mercy] uttered as a war cry. French Creole was once the language of Trinidad and Tobago's African population, and in this language "*sans humanité*" is rendered as " *santi manité*" or sometimes as "*sani manité*." The latter form is the one which the West Indian intellectual heard most often. He thus opted for that form as the defining title of his first novel. The spelling he used was *Sanni Mannitae*.

In 1994, there occurred one of those moments of confluence between preparation and opportunity. The West Indian intellectual founded a commercial publishing enterprise called Original World Press. The first work published by this self-empowering enterprise was *Sanni Mannitae*.

Even as his first novel was making its way through the

publication process, the West Indian intellectual was working on a book that would document the African origin of Hispanic culture and civilization. The manuscript was first submitted to Howard University Press. They, however, deemed that its focus was too narrow for the Capstone. The manuscript was then sent for consideration to the University of Missouri Press. Their reader advised against publication by a university press, but he recommended submission to a commercial press. He reasoned that controversial theses such as the one presented in the manuscript were more appropriate in books from a commercial press.

The manuscript was then submitted to Karia Press in London, England. This small press was Black owned and had earned a reputation for publishing very progressive material. Karia sent the manuscript out to reviewers, who recommended publication. By this time the West Indian intellectual had himself become the owner of a small Black owned press. He felt that it would make more sense for the book to be published by Original World Press, for he would have complete control over every aspect of the process. Accordingly, he informed his colleague at Karia of his decision to pull the manuscript. Karia was disappointed, but the decision was irrevocable. And in September 1996, the manuscript, which had been circulating among publishing houses for about five years, finally appeared in print as *Amazing Connections: Kemet to Hispanophone Africana Literature* under the imprint of Original World Press.

True to its stated mission to give voice to those who have been excluded from the inner circles of the Eurocentric Academy, Original World Press issued in 1999 the book, *Panriga: Tacarigua's Contribution to the Evolution of the Steelband Phenomenon in Trinidad and Tobago*, by Kenrick P. Thomas. Thomas is a nontraditional scholar, a man who became directly involved with steelband music from the very beginning. It is worthy of note that this Thomas comes from the same region of the small Caribbean island as did John Jacob Thomas, the self-made scholar who was born in the immediate post-Emancipation period.

The blurb on the back cover of *Panriga* asserts:

> It amounts to a Declaration of Emancipation by a descendant of Africans, and, most appropriately, it was launched in Trinidad in 1999 during the Emancipation Day festival. The work establishes masterfully the connectedness of Trinbagonian culture to "Mother Africa," proffering a firsthand account of the development of an art form that is peculiar to the two-island nation. In fact, the author declares decisively and insistently that steelband music developed from the Orisha tradition. Many are the forces at work today trying to wrest from Trinbagonian Africans the ownership of their peculiar cultural expressions, so a book like *Panriga* is timely. Original World Press stands firmly with Thomas and all the thousands, indeed, millions of *cimarrones* who have stood up to be counted.

The fourth book published by Original World Press was *Ah Come Back Home: Perspectives on the Trinidad and Tobago Carnival*. This work appeared in February 2000, barely in time for that year's Carnival. It was launched at the Heritage Hall of the Trinidad and Tobago Public Library in Port-of-Spain in the week before Carnival. The back cover describes the book as follows:

> This volume marks a radical departure in the study of Carnival and a distinct addition to knowledge and understanding of this important area of life in the African Diaspora. In beginning at the beginning, the contributors almost always move beyond the regular misrepresentation of the festival as a creation of Europeans. The contributors are all both highly trained and experienced in several

relevant fields. Some are practicing academics; all are long-standing initiates and intellectuals of the beloved festival. The resulting work is not merely informative, but also authoritative, challenging, and stimulating. Carnival practitioners, government officials, students, and, indeed, the general public will find this volume essential, perhaps indispensable.

Within six weeks of the September 11, 2001 tragedy, the West Indian intellectual had completed a book-length manuscript on the event. By the end of December 2001, the manuscript had been published as *Willie Lynch to the World Trade Center: An African American Response to Nine-One-One.* Freedom of the press is guaranteed only to those who own one. The publication of this book was an exercise not only of freedom of the press but of African self-affirmation, as the back cover text proclaims:

> Many African Americans perished on September 11, 2001, Nine-One-One, victims of international terrorism. Many African Americans perished in the federal building in Oklahoma City, victims of domestic terrorism. Countless millions of Africans perished in the trans-Atlantic slave trade, a crime against humanity. Frederick Douglass shows that whites employed systematic terrorism in order to "maintain rule and order upon the plantation." African Americans still continue to perish as victims of this institutionalized terrorism. African Americans, attentive to their cultural traditions, which go back to the beginning of recorded history, have developed a nonviolent, "We Shall Overcome" response to terrorism. It is time for all Americans, and, indeed, for all humanity to profit from the secular wisdom of Black folks.

In spring 2001, Original World Press gave voice to a new Jamaican poet, Louis Alexander Hemans, when it published his first book, *Midnight Moods, Morning Metaphors*. Hemans earned the B.A. and two M.A. degrees from the Capstone. He has completed all but his dissertation for the Ph.D. in Spanish at the Capstone. However, since Hemans' mentor is the West Indian intellectual, the Jamaican poet has found his path to the doctorate strewn with obstacles placed there by hostile African American administrators. It could be reasonably concluded that these latter consider the Affirmative Action Program in higher education to be a license to promote the narrow self-interest of a tiny group of African Americans.

The West Indian intellectual achieved the highest forms of self-affirmation without any help from the Affirmative Action Program in higher education. This self-determination is the only responsible response to the affirmative action of white male privilege/entitlement, which has always been the bedrock of Western societies. The evidence suggests that there has developed at the Capstone a practice of replacing the ages-old tradition of the affirmative action of white male privilege/entitlement with African American privilege/entitlement. This practice appears to be a direct consequence and manifestation of the corruption of the Affirmative Action Program in higher education.

CHAPTER FOUR

The West Indian Intellectual v the Capstone

Hay aves que cruzan el pantano
Y no se manchan.
Mi plumaje es de esos.
SALVADOR DÍAZ MIRÓN

Historically Black Colleges and Universities (HBCUs) were set up by the federal government right after the abolition of slavery to provide higher education for Negroes. They are, as the name indicates, race-based institutions established under a prototype of the Affirmative Action Program. In the present political climate they have become an anachronism. However, since they exist now and have always existed at the margin of white civil society, they enjoy the protection of the federal government even in the present climate of hostility to the Affirmative Action Program. Howard is the pride and joy of these HBCUs, receiving much of its funding from federal government appropriations. Relative to its student body population, Howard is one of the most generously federally funded institutions in the entire country. Indeed, the Howard University president with an annual salary of about six hundred thousand dollars (reported for 2001) is one of the highest paid university presidents in the entire nation.

The Howard University administration interprets the mandate of the HBCU narrowly, limiting its concern exclusively to Blacks born in the United States. Again, because the HBCUs are deemed to be marginal, this spirit of reverse discrimination has tended to be winked at by the federal government. The problem is that in the post Civil Rights era the cream of the black population born in the United States has been siphoned off to the better white institutions. Thus the majority of the black student body in the graduate programs at Howard University are foreign born Blacks with great numbers from the English-speaking Caribbean (West Indies). The West Indies is also over represented in the black faculty at the university. Two decades ago, a Howard University official expressed in confidence his concern that in the College of Arts and Sciences seventy-five percent of the full professors were white. This situation would not have changed significantly over the years.

The evidence suggests that African Americans routinely attain positions of authority at Howard solely on the basis of the narrow interpretation of the Affirmative Action Program in higher education. It is not surprising, then, that from time to time they would dare to discriminate even against Whites. This has led to reverse discrimination lawsuits, which have almost always resulted in a loss for the Blacks in authority at Howard. Blacks from the English-speaking Caribbean perceive themselves to be the more customary targets of the discriminatory action of the native born Blacks who control Howard University. The former, however, have been hesitant to file discrimination charges against fellow Blacks.

The situation of the specific West Indian intellectual on whom this book is focused is, then, representative. An extremely well-qualified scholar, he chose Howard University because he was unfamiliar with the peculiar problems of the HBCUs. He rose rapidly through the ranks by virtue of his impressive scholarly production. By the time this current book is on the shelves, he will have written twelve books and authored over seventy other publications. His work in Hispanic, Caribbean, and African literatures has earned national and international recognition. For this reason he poses a threat to the national Blacks who control Howard University.

The Complaint

After twenty-five years of trying to work out his problems in house, the West Indian intellectual finally, in January 2002, filed suit in the Washington D.C. District Court against Howard University. The complaint alleged discrimination on the basis of national origin, religion, and in retaliation. The major harm suffered was in the area of salary. In spite of his sterling contributions in the three established areas of teaching, research, and service, the West Indian intellectual was denied merit increases under the new system set in place by the president of the university. In addition, the West Indian intellectual for two decades sought unsuccessfully the chairmanship of his department.

The first competitor to win the position of chair during the period in question was another West Indian intellectual. When this scholar was summarily relieved of his post, he was replaced by a significantly less qualified African American male, who, although holding the rank of full professor of French, had never earned a doctorate in French nor had even demonstrated any particular expertise in French or Francophone studies. Indeed, the decision to anoint to the chairmanship this singularly unqualified faculty member appears to have been taken by the very same administrator who is supposed to have been responsible for firing Stanley A. Cyrus. All of the chairs appointed subsequently have been African Americans and have not evinced any particular competence.

The West Indian intellectual maintains that, inspired by his religious beliefs, he has sought to live a virtuous life as a heterosexual, monogamous male. He comes across, then, as not condoning promiscuity, neither heterosexual nor homosexual. As such he is at odds with the prevailing culture of an institution which takes pride in having Alain Leroy Locke as one of its guiding lights. In her book, *Color, Sex, and Poetry in the Harlem Renaissance,* Gloria T. Hull, a well-respected scholar, who happens to be African American, examines Locke's heritage. She describes Locke as:

> A Harvard-trained Ph.D., Rhodes scholar, and Howard University philosophy professor [who] gave definitive shape to "the New Negro" in his 1925 anthology of that name. More importantly, his smooth, learned manner inspired patrons to make him a conduit for their largesse to black artists. Thus, Locke dispensed not only money but also advice, support, and vital aid to many needful young writers. His handling of his role was controversial, but no one denied its centrality. (7)

Hull declares baldly: "The problem with Locke, however, is that he behaved misogynistically and actively favored men" (7). The College of Arts and Sciences of Howard University is sited in Locke Hall. There is a picture of the great man proudly displayed in the main entry foyer to the building named after him.

It is interesting that the picture of Locke is a black and white one in a twenty-two-by-twenty-six-inch frame. However, presiding over the grand main staircase of the Founder's Library hangs an imposing portrait of an old white man decked out in a Civil War general's uniform. He is Oliver Otis Howard, the beneficent founder of the Capstone. The good general was famed for his role in "pacifying" the aboriginal peoples of the North American continent. He was an avid buffalo hunter, and, hence, generation after generation of Howard students have proudly proclaimed the bison as their totem. No one stops to consider that the wanton slaughter of buffalo brought irreparable harm not only to the native people but to the very ecology of our continent.

Howard University is proud of its founder. It proudly bears his name. The institution is equally proud of the "founder" of the Harlem Renaissance. It proudly names after him the building which houses the College of Arts and Sciences. And this building is just across the quadrangle from Douglass Hall, named after Frederick Douglass, of whom the institution is justly proud. However, Douglass was not connected with the Capstone in the same way in which Howard and Locke were.

Hull is an African American, but putting scholarly objectivity above racial solidarity, she declares:

> Locke's behavior becomes even more problematic because of his obvious partiality toward young males, to whom he was sexually attracted. Locke, in fact, functioned within a homosexual coterie of friendship and patronage that suggests that literary events were, in more than a few instances, tied to "bedroom politics" and "sexual croneyism"—as they no doubt may have been in the heterosexual world also. (8)

Not willing to engage in "bedroom politics" because of his religious beliefs, the West Indian intellectual alleges that he was excluded from the inner circles of an organization which functioned in the tradition of its most acclaimed guiding light, Alain Leroy Locke.

The West Indian intellectual came to the defense of a younger West Indian scholar, Mary A. Harris, whom he considered to have suffered the double blast of Locke-style misogynism coupled with African American xenophobia. Harris earned the Ph.D. in Spanish from the University of Oklahoma. However, she was denied tenure and promotion at the same time that the Capstone promoted to the rank of associate professor of Spanish an African American male who had not even completed all of the requirements for the doctorate in foreign language education. In fact, the Capstone had in the very year in which this African American male finished this non-qualifying doctorate not only promoted him but had made him chair of the Department of Romance Languages.

Harris might have been successful in overcoming the double burden of her gender and her national origin if she had been prepared to engage in, or at least overtly condone, the Locke brand of "bedroom politics." Not only was Harris unprepared to take these steps, but she made the fatal error of incurring the envy of her African American colleagues when as a single woman still in probationary rank she purchased her own home. The Capstone will rush to point out that there is another Black female foreign-born faculty member who affirmed herself by becoming a home owner in spite of being single. However, this individual is decidedly not a West Indian intellectual, and apparently has not evinced any particular disapproval of the homosexual lifestyle.

Envy evinced by the colleagues was given administrative relevance in a written communication by a chair of the Department of Modern Languages and Literatures at the Capstone. In January 1999, this chair wrote to the Dean of the College that the West Indian intellectual should not be "permitted" to travel to Trinidad and Tobago for the purposes of pursuing his research on Carnival because this trip would "create a morale problem" within the Department. The chair explained that the West Indian intellectual's colleagues considered his research trips to Trinidad at Carnival time to be "an annual winter holiday."

The Capstone considers itself a research institution type one, in the same league as Harvard, Yale, Duke, etc. The West Indian intellectual by 1999 had demonstrated unflagging interest and considerable success in his research activities. Between 1977 and 1999, the Capstone had helped to finance only one of the West Indian intellectual's trips to Carnival. This was in 1978. If, in these circumstances, a chair could in a written communication cite the envy of colleagues as grounds for opposing the research activity of a senior colleague, it is not unreasonable to conclude that this same kind of envy factored into the Capstone's decision not to promote and tenure Harris.

The chair's opposition on the grounds of envy to the West Indian intellectual's trip prevailed. It is reasonable to conclude that African Americans at the Capstone also resented the West Indian intellectual's success as a homeowner. In fact, as will be shown later on in this chapter, one of the issues raised by the attorneys for the Capstone was precisely the West Indian intellectual's economic situation. In any case, the West Indian intellectual alleges in his complaint that the Capstone took negative action towards him partly in retaliation for his coming to Harris's defense.

The Capstone's Response

The world of litigation is not for the squeamish, the faint of heart. It is the arena of the *argumentum ad hominem* and, especially, the *argumentum ad baculum.* And true to its custom, the Capstone came out with a big stick [*baculum*] for the West Indian *homo*. (It should be pointed out that the term *homo* is used here as the nominative case of the Latin noun, which was employed in the preceding sentence in its accusative case form, *hominem.*) The University laid out its case in the course of the ten hours of sworn testimony taken from the West Indian intellectual as part of discovery. The Capstone, charged with discrimination, responded by attempting to show that it had acted properly in withholding the West Indian intellectual's merit increase and in denying him the chairmanship of his department.

In the course of the 1997 merit increase competition, the same chair, who in January 1999 would declare in an official written communication that faculty envy was a relevant consideration, wrote a secret memorandum to the central administration accusing the West Indian intellectual of disloyalty to the Capstone. This chair put in writing to the central administration that the West Indian intellectual had an impressive record of publications, but that this should not be sufficient to earn a merit increase. According to the chair in his secret memo, in addition to his disloyalty to the Capstone, the West Indian intellectual had failed to keep office hours, had rarely attended faculty meetings, and had steadfastly refused to serve on committees. All of these were merely unproven allegations. The chair made no attempt whatsoever to document his charges. In fact, as it turned out, the allegation of disloyalty was based on remarks the West Indian intellectual was supposed to have made two decades earlier.

Even if any of the accusations proved to be consistent with fact, they were totally irrelevant to the merit process as it is normally carried out in the mainstream Academy. The president of the Capstone accepted the chair's presentation and denied the West Indian intellectual a merit increase, notwithstanding the fact that his book, *Amazing Connections*, had been published during the period for which merit was being considered. Some have argued that the president would jump at any opportunity to deny merit to a faculty or staff member so as to ensure a brimming pot from which to award himself extremely generous pay increases. The fact is that the Capstone clung doggedly to its position, supporting its decision by repeating on every occasion the unproven and outrageous allegations first made by the chair. This unqualified African American, as was suggested earlier on, had been appointed to the position on the basis of the corrupt interpretation of the Affirmative Action Program.

The unqualified but anointed African American chair, in the first year of his tenure, added to the list of ridiculous allegations against the West Indian intellectual the charge of missing an excessive number of classes and the charge of awarding an excessive number of As. Characteristically, the charges were presented simply as observations made by the chair, without the slightest attempt at verification through the normal investigative processes. Once these absurd allegations were made, the Capstone regarded them as proven fact. Therefore, they surfaced in discovery as part of the Capstone's justification of the discriminatory actions taken against the West Indian intellectual.

Not shying away from the appearance of inconsistency, the Capstone's lawyers charged the West Indian intellectual with making disparaging remarks about the academic acumen of African American students. The lawyers are handsomely paid by the

Capstone and simply ignore any of the ugly realities of life at the HBCUs. It is not uncommon to encounter at these HBCUs, and the Capstone is no exception, white faculty members who have a fundamentally *faut de mieux* attitude towards their job. Such faculty members not only consider their African American students to be academically disadvantaged, but declare so openly. If the highly paid lawyers for the Capstone had been properly briefed by their client—and the president of the university is an attorney himself—they would not have articulated such nonsensical charges against the West Indian intellectual.

Of course, the Capstone did not inform its lawyers that in the minutes of a meeting of the tenured faculty members of the Department of Modern Languages and Literatures in fall 1999 the view is expressed that the upper administration of the Capstone is so inefficient that failure to adhere to rules and regulations can at times be a remedy. The referenced failure to comply to rules and regulations was, in fact, a series of irregularities committed by the chair of the Department in an attempt to short circuit the process for appointing a faculty member on the tenure track. The unconventional actions included the forging of a signature on an official document and the reporting on the same document of a vote which never took place. The majority faction of the Department's tenured faculty held the central administration in such low esteem that it deemed the actions of the chair to be acceptable.

All of the discussion referenced in the preceding paragraph took place in the context of what must be seen as a revolt staged by the chair and the majority faction of the tenured faculty. When the indiscretions of the chair came to the attention of the central administration of the Capstone, they opted for a slap on the wrist, forcing the African American, who had been anointed by them just two years earlier in pursuance of their interpretation of the

Affirmative Action Program, to resign. Emboldened by the support of the majority faction of the tenured members and by his own understandable misunderstanding of the role of a chair in Academe, the forger refused to demit. He continued to occupy the office space designated for the departmental chair, although he had been stripped of his authority. So the Department was left chair-less for a period.

The central administration of the Capstone finally persuaded the rebellious professor to clear his "things" out of the chair's office. His place was taken by another African American who had been anointed earlier. It should be noted that the rebellious chair, who deemed the forging of a signature and the filing of false documents to be mere peccadillos justified by his ultimately laudable intentions, is the very one who introduced into the official record a series of defamatory comments about the West Indian intellectual.

The lawyers for the Capstone indicated in discovery that their client was justified in moving to compress the West Indian intellectual's salary because the latter had been enriching himself through his publishing enterprise. The West Indian intellectual's involvement in publishing was not seen by the Capstone as an act of African self-affirmation, but rather as a manifestation of West Indian arrogance and selfishness. To make their case, the lawyers for the Capstone insisted on seeing the West Indian intellectual's tax returns for the years 1997 to 2002. They had been told of the "annual winter vacations" and the "mansion in Adelphi" (as the West Indian intellectual's home had been described by some envious African American colleagues), and they were confident that the tax returns would give evidence of significant outside income. They hoped that these documents might reveal some violations of the tax code or of the Capstone's rules and regulations.

At one point in the deposition, the lead lawyer for the Capstone declared dramatically with the appropriate gesture and tone that, in fact, the West Indian intellectual had suffered a nervous breakdown in the spring of 1998. The lawyer's face glowed with triumph as he slammed down what he deemed to be his trump card against the West Indian. The Capstone's lawyer was trying to make the case that the West Indian was a neurotic suffering from the Obsessive Compulsive Disorder, rendering him unfit for any administrative duties and barely able to perform his duties as an instructor. Thus evidence of a debilitating nervous breakdown as a consequence of which he missed an inordinate number of classes, thereby depriving his students of the instruction for which they had paid, would considerably weaken the West Indian's case.

When all else fails, there is always sex. Most assuredly the Capstone's attorneys must have searched high and low for some sex scandal with which to sully the West Indian intellectual's reputation. They cleverly paved the way to the major accusation by having the West Indian intellectual read the sex scene from his latest novel, *Spoiled Priest*. The lawyer, again with the appropriate histrionics, taxed to the fullest his abilities in literary analysis declaring the entire novel to be "trashy." Since there is a psychological component to literary criticism, the lawyer proffered the opinion that the West Indian intellectual's creative writings manifested an inordinate preoccupation with sexual fantasies. This view was probably developed in collaboration with the colleague who authored the e-mail message which will be discussed later.

Whereas literary criticism is not expected to be the forte of a lawyer, the application of basic logic is. The Capstone's lawyer made another foray into the analysis of the West Indian intellectual's writing with even more disastrous results, for this time his logic was patently weak. He cornered the West Indian intellectual into declaring that anyone who would put in writing the view that the Nine-One-One tragedy was a good thing could not be considered for an administrative position at the Capstone. Then, with the usual sophomoric flourish, he had the West Indian intellectual read the following sentence from his book, *Willie Lynch to the World Trade Center: An African American Response to Nine-One-One*: "There is a good side to the senseless slaughter" (139).

The breakdown in logic associated with the efforts at literary criticism on the part of the Capstone's lawyer is consistent with the contradictions in the reasoning both of the Expert Witness (this is the subject matter of chapter 5) and the Capstone itself. The thrust of the lightly literate lawyer's rejection of the "trashy" novel was the belief that it was not germane to the West Indian intellectual's discipline, precisely the language used by the Capstone's chief academic accuser. In the same year in which the chair of the Department forged a colleague's signature and reported falsely about a vote of the colleagues, he declared in a written communication that the West Indian intellectual's research on Carnival was not "germane to his discipline."

Carnival studies is a field included under the umbrella of cultural studies, and cultural studies has become the hot field of the literary studies complex. The Department of Modern Languages and Literatures is part of the Humanities Division of the Capstone. For this reason faculty members in the Department routinely teach courses in world literature. The West Indian intellectual has routinely been assigned to teach such courses, which—as even a functionally literate lawyer must know—involve the teaching of novels. *Spoiled Priest* and *Sanni Mannitae* could legitimately be included as part of the subject matter of such courses. The Expert Witness manifested a significant lapse in expertise when he expressed the view that the West Indian's creative literary activities were not germane to his function as professor of Spanish in the Department of Modern Languages and Literatures at Howard University.

Furthermore, the Expert Witness overlooked the fact that the second highest paid faculty member of the Department is an African American anointed to the full professorship of French even though his training and expertise lie in a field not generally included within the areas covered under the umbrella of French. This field is foreign language education, and neither is it included under the humanities umbrella. The year in which the chair declared that research in Carnival was not germane to Spanish was the very same year in which he committed a series of gross irregularities in order to hire on the tenure track as an assistant professor of French an individual who did not have a Ph.D. in French. That individual is an African American, and her Ph.D. in applied linguistics was earned at a university which also granted the Ph.D. in French. It could be concluded, then, that this individual was anointed to an assistant professorship of French at the Capstone through the perverted interpretation of the Affirmative Action Program.

The Capstone's lawyer argued that the West Indian intellectual had an overdeveloped libido manifest in the sexual fantasies portrayed in his "trashy" novels. But that was only the tip of the iceberg according to the Capstone's lawyers. The fact was that under cover of carrying out research on the Carnival festival, the West Indian intellectual traveled down to his home country on a yearly escapade to cavort with his girlfriends. One of these girlfriends was the focus of the interest of the University attorneys. To ensure the maximum possible damage, the University attorneys insisted on deposing the West Indian intellectual's spouse of twenty-five years. The only purpose served by this deposition was that of giving the University attorneys the chance to confront the West Indian intellectual's spouse with the accusations of sexual impropriety. It was hoped that such a presentation might have triggered an angry response in the West Indian intellectual's spouse and lead to damaging revelations.

Although any slipping away to Carnival with an "outside woman" would have absolutely no relevance to the case, it could destroy the marriage between the West Indian intellectual and his spouse of twenty-five years. Ian Isidore and Juana Isidra, two West Indians, one from the islands, the other from Central America, had met and fallen in love as students at UCLA. They had the same name, they had the same cultural background, they were made for each other. Their first date occurred on Thanksgiving Day, 1973. It was also Juana' birthday. Ian Isidore came to the Capstone in 1977. Juana Isidra was still completing her M.A. at UCLA.

After a five-year courtship Ian Isidore and Juana Isidra gave themselves to each other for all eternity at a Nuptial Mass celebrated in the Andrew Rankin Chapel of the Capstone on December 23, 1978. The Roman Catholic chaplain of the Capstone, an African American, was the officiating priest. The gospel choir from St. Benedict the Moor Roman Catholic church provided appropriate Afrocentric liturgical music. Both Ian Isidore and Juana Isidra have taken their marriage vows with the utmost seriousness. Their union has been blessed with two children, a girl, Monifa Isidra, who was born on August 30, 1982, and a boy, Isidore Kamau, who was born on December 3, 1988.

In contemporary North American society, only two of five marriages survive. By the grace of God, Ian Isidore and Juana Isidra will celebrate their twenty-fifth wedding anniversary on December 23, 2003. This marriage is triumphantly Pan-African, Pan-Caribbean, and Pan-Christian—Ian Isidore is Roman Catholic and Juana Isidra is a born-again Christian. Every African, every human being, should have an interest in helping this marriage to continue to work forever.

What goes around comes around. On the society page of *The Washington Post* of April 25, 2003, there appeared an item by Lloyd Grove under the headline: "News from Splitsville." The piece begins flippantly: "Spring has sprung, and divorce is in the air." And continues:

> In Washington, Howard University President **Patrick Swygert** and his wife, **Sonja**, are preparing to end their 33-year marriage that produced two sons. ... Their respective attorneys told us yesterday that they legally separated last month ... Sonja filed the original complaint in November, and associates of the couple told us that they frequently have been overheard arguing. Sonja's attorney ... told us: "She wants to resolve this amicably and quickly, and hopes it goes uncontested." Patrick's lawyer ... said: "With all due respect, it's our policy to not comment on cases." (C3)

The lawyer representing the president in this very personal matter of his marriage invoked "all due respect." At the same time the lawyer representing the president in the very public matter of a complaint against the Capstone for discrimination on the basis of national origin did not hesitate to disregard the respect due the West Indian intellectual. For this lawyer callously tried to push the West Indian intellectual's marriage to the very rocks on which the union of Patrick and Sonja had met its demise. *The Washington Post* harkened to the plea of Patrick's lawyer and did not reveal the content of Sonja's original complaint. Since such complaints are a matter of public record, the juicy details should be available for the asking at the District of Columbia Superior Court.

The "Jungle Fever" Factor

The Capstone's lawyers, in preparing their defense, interviewed many of the West Indian intellectual's colleagues. Some of these colleagues supplied what they considered salacious information, damaging to the colleague they deemed to be the least collegial. In her eagerness to do harm, one such colleague committed a fundamental indiscretion of creating a self-incriminating written document. The document, an e-mail message, is reproduced herewith in its entirety, except that in the interest of discretion the names of the hostile Howard University faculty members have been redacted as follows: the writer of the letter, a white female born in the United States, is called Dr. Jane Doe-Deeay and her special colleague, a black foreign born female, is called Dr. Jane Doe-Knocktay.

> 2 MAR 2003
>
> Dr. Smart: I am not gay, but I am a very private person. Before the 19th of March 2003, please have your lawyer inform the university lawyers that you are deleting from any and all aspects of your lawsuit against the university any and all statements or allusions, direct or indirect, regarding my sexuality, Dr. Doe-Knocktay's sexuality and Dr. Doe-Knocktay's daughter. Failing that, I shall file a statement with the university lawyers that your perverse allegations are a direct result of my refusal to yield to your sexual proposition made to me on the night I attended your presentation in Trinidad. I was surprised at the time, and mentioned the incident to a colleague at the conference the next day, but decided to take no

action. I dismissed it as a mere misjudgment on your part and had no desire to bring pain to you or your family for such an indiscretion. However, I now see it as part of a plan to retaliate against me—a posteriori, if your allegation was filed after the conference, a priori, if your allegation was filed before the conference, in a sick attempt to "get" me one way or another, whether I yielded or did not yield to your intention that we "get to know each other as a man and a woman." That was when I understood why my request to Wayne to ask someone to call me a cab had resulted in a discussion with you about who would drive me back to the hotel. I should have been suspicious, but I was not. If I had not unwittingly given you the opportunity, I guess you would have created it somehow. Of course, your first novel shows that such a plan forms part of your imaginary. In addition, your proposition and vengeful allegations fit the pattern of attack/rapproachment toward me that is very well documented.

You have, in your twisted view of people, misinterpreted many things and are ignorant of others. I live 30 miles from campus, and the drive takes an hour. When I have classes or work until late in the day—this semester, my Tuesday seminar goes until 7:30 p.m.—I am often too tired to drive home safely. Several people have offered their homes to me, should I wish to stay in the city. I occasionally stay at Dr. Doe-Knocktay's, which gives me the chance to be with her daughter, who is my goddaughter, a responsibility that I take seriously, since her godfather and I swore before Almighty God and a Roman Catholic congregation to love her and care for her as if she were our own child. I am one of several caregivers for the child and for her grandmother when Dr. Doe-Knocktay has evening engagements, some of which are dates with a male friend. You are surprisingly ignorant, for a married man, to not know that women's gynecological records contain ample evidence of heterosexual activity.

Both my colleague and I can demonstrate that your depraved

> allegations are false, but I would prefer that we not have to. Withdraw them, or I shall be forced to come forward. What you do with other parts of your lawsuit is not of particular interest to me.

In fall 2002, Doe-Deeay had, in fact, visited Trinidad and Tobago for the first time in her life in order to participate in a conference on Latin American and Caribbean studies. The West Indian intellectual was also participating in this conference, however, unlike Doe-Deeay, he was not reimbursed by the Capstone for his travel. As was his custom, the West Indian intellectual made it a point to share his scholarship with the general public of his native land. His trips home for Carnival have always included speaking engagements to the general public or appearances on Trinidad and Tobago television. In the case of the fall 2002 visit, he had been invited to speak at the Paragon Sports and Cultural Club. His lecture was open to the general public and was a continuation of the theme presented on earlier return visits to his native land, namely, the classical African roots of the Trinidad and Tobago Carnival.

The conference itself was sited at the St. Augustine Campus of the University of the West Indies, located about ten miles to the east of Port-of-Spain. The Paragon Sports and Cultural Club is located in an upscale western suburb of the city. Doe-Deeay did the West Indian intellectual the courtesy of attending his talk. Unfamiliar with the island's public transportation system, she arrived late. However, the West Indian intellectual stopped in the middle of his presentation to welcome his colleague, who was given a round of applause by the audience. She was the only white person in that group of over fifty people.

The West Indian intellectual, one of twelve children, is a scion of a prominent Trinidad and Tobago family. His brother Wayne, now a prominent attorney, had been in his youth a soccer star as well as a cricketer. Indeed, he had once been a member of the national cricket team and, as such, would have been a bona fide local hero, according to V. S. Naipaul. Wayne served as the president of the Paragon Sports and Cultural Club.

After the lecture, a group of officials of the club repaired to the bar for refreshments. At about ten thirty, Doe-Deeay asked Wayne to call her a cab to take her back to her hotel. For a female colleague visiting the island for the first time to be allowed to get into a taxi at 10:30 p.m. to head back to the Hilton Hotel was out of the question. Wayne, did, in fact, offer to drive Doe-Deeay back to the Hilton, but it was a weekday, and he had to go to work the next day. The West Indian intellectual did have a car at his disposal. Doe-Deeay was his colleague and, as such, was his guest; so he drove her back to the hotel.

The West Indian intellectual declared on two occasions under oath at his deposition that since December 23, 1978 his wife has been his only sexual partner. This declaration was made under oath and is not to be equated with the notorious finger-wagging "I did not have sex with that woman." The West Indian intellectual has been to Trinidad for Carnival on numerous occasions. He has had many, many opportunities to "get to know very attractive women in Trinidad and Tobago as *a man and a woman*." In fact, the Capstone's lawyers were convinced that he was having an affair with at least one of these attractive women who also go to Trinidad for Carnival. However, the West Indian intellectual, a former monk and seminarian, has always sought to avoid "occasions of sin." It can be affirmed without hesitation that taking Doe-Deeay back to her hotel was not even remotely close to an "occasion of sin."

Doe-Deeay's allegations are pure fabrication and are simply preposterous. At first sight, it appears that she just lost her grip on reality. However, upon careful consideration there emerges an alarming connection, which casts a disturbing light on Doe-Deeay's wild accusations. In his *Notes on the State of Virginia*, Thomas Jefferson has a chapter on "Laws," in which he discusses, among other topics, the matter of race relations. Jefferson argues for a rigid separation between Whites and Blacks and posits his position on, among other considerations, "the real distinction which nature has made" between Whites and Blacks. Jefferson continues:

> The first difference which strikes us is that of colour. . . . And is this difference of no importance? Is it not the foundation of a greater or less share of beauty in the two races? Are not the fine mixtures of red and white, the expressions of every passion by greater or less suffusions of colour in the one, preferable to that eternal monotony, which reigns in the countenances, that immoveable veil of black which covers all the emotions of the other race? Add to these, flowing hair, a more elegant symmetry of form, *their own judgment in favour of the whites, declared by their preference of them, as uniformly as is the preference of the Oran-ootan for the black women over those of his own species.* (138 emphasis added)

Doe-Deeay appears, like Jefferson, to take it as self-evident that every white woman—no matter what her age, state of health, level of physical pulchritude—is desirable to a black man.

Doe-Deeay drew attention in her correspondence to the fact that she lives thirty miles from the Capstone. Indeed, she does come from the state of Maryland, the very state in which Frederick Douglass was enslaved. Indeed, it is conceivable that some of the barbaric white folks singled out in Douglass's autobiographical accounts may have been Doe-Deeay's direct ancestors. Edward

Covey (see chapter five) could very well have been Doe-Deeay's great grandfather. It appears, too, that Doe-Deeay deems it necessary to "dumb down" the curriculum in order to facilitate the learning experience of her African American students at the Capstone.

Doe-Deeay is someone who considers herself a sophisticated player in the game of administrative intrigue, but she was extraordinarily careless in concocting her extortion plan. In the first place, extortion is a criminal offense. Then Doe-Deeay failed to take into account the fact of the West Indian intellectual's unimpeachable marital fidelity. This being the case, his alleged (and outrageously stilted) invitation to Doe-Deeay would amount not to an indiscretion, but rather to an act of either incomprehensible self-debasement or of heroic generosity. It would have meant that he had decided to initiate his life as an adulterer with a sexual partner who is probably the least attractive female on the Howard University campus, a woman who is the quintessential Plain Jane.

Whether Doe-Deeay is gay or not makes no difference to the West Indian intellectual. Doe-Knocktay's mating habits are similarly of no concern to him. As to the matter of Doe-Deeay's "gynecological record," he finds the topic utterly, in fact, painfully, distasteful. In any case, it is not germane to the litigation. What is germane is the fact that between 1997 and 2002, Doe-Knocktay, without having written a single book was awarded a salary increase of more than twenty-two thousand dollars. During that same period, the West Indian intellectual wrote three books on different topics. His salary was increased by about seven thousand dollars. There must be some reason for such a gross disparity. It is prudent to consider national origin and sexual preference as the bases for this disparity. Doe-Knocktay is of European national origin. She is, indeed, black, but so too are African Americans, the beneficiaries of the particular form of Affirmative Action practiced at the Capstone.

Furthermore, the external evidence indicates that there exists a special relationship between Doe-Deeay and Doe-Knocktay. In the 1995-96 academic year, the West Indian intellectual drew attention to the inconsistency of the department's Appointments Promotion and Tenure Committee with regard to the tenure applications of Doe-Deeay and Effie Boldridge. This latter is an African American female, who earned the Ph.D. in Spanish from the University of Missouri-Columbia in 1970. Doe-Deeay began her appointment at the Capstone as an instructor working on her Ph.D from the University of Maryland College Park. She barely completed the doctorate in time to beat the clock on her probationary appointment.

Doe-Knocktay took it upon herself to come to Doe-Deeay's defense with a virulent *ad hominen* attack on the West Indian intellectual. Doe-Knocktay's actions came as a complete surprise to him, and the only reasonable explanation he could find for them lay in the special relationship between herself and Doe-Deeay. Until Doe-Knocktay unleashed her venom upon the West Indian intellectual, her relationship with Doe-Deeay was an entirely personal matter. However, since it appears to have triggered Doe-Knocktay's response to a professional assessment of Doe-Deeay's qualifications vis-à-vis Boldridge's, the relationship was brought into the public sphere.

In fall 2003, the Doe-Deeay-Doe-Knocktay partnership in the campaign to destroy the West Indian intellectual brought the Capstone into an even lower state of disrepute. The counsel representing the University in Smart v Howard filed before the United States District Court for the District of Columbia a motion to reopen discovery for a limited purpose. The memorandum in support of the motion affirms:

> The extension of discovery will permit defendant to investigate the source of threatening and intimidating calls made to a key witness on the evening immediately following her deposition testimony in this case. Such discovery is needed (1) to prevent future efforts to tamper with witnesses, and (2) to support a motion for sanctions if the requested discovery establishes that plaintiff was involved either directly or indirectly.

Doe-Knocktay had given sworn testimony which she believed was harmful to the West Indian intellectual's case. That very night she "answered her telephone at home and 'heard a heavily accented male voice mumbling' unclear words, and she hung up." Counsel for the Capstone goes on to declare:

> Approximately twenty minutes later, Dr. Doe-Knocktay received another call at her home, and a heavily accented male voice stated: "[Y]ou will soon die." Dr. Doe-Knocktay immediately hung up the phone and left it off the hook for the remainder of the night.

Doe-Knocktay is a native speaker of French. Although she is a full professor of French, she never completed the Ph.D. in French. She is not a reliable authority on accents in English, and probably not in French either. The West Indian intellectual is a native speaker of standard Caribbean English. His English is essentially the same as that of Roy L. Austin, the West Indian intellectual who was appointed by President George W. Bush to serve as the United States ambassador to Trinidad and Tobago. His English is essentially the same as that of Derek Walcott, who gained the Nobel Prize for literature.

West Indians may be foreign Blacks, but their native language is not a foreign one. Doe-Knocktay is a European national. She is a foreign Black, but one whose mother tongue is French, a foreign language. Afrocentric intellectuals argue that all Blacks are Africans, a position which is not espoused by the leadership of the Capstone. However, for the purposes of this lawsuit, the Capstone seeks to suspend all distinctions between Blacks who were born outside of the United States. They want to suck and blow at the same time.

Doe-Knocktay deems the West Indian intellectual's English to be heavily accented, and the lightly literate lawyer representing the Capstone has accepted her analysis. He has also accepted her characterization of the deposition testimony. For he asserts:

> At her deposition, Dr. Doe-Knocktay explained her own achievements, and disputed plaintiff's attempts to diminish her accomplishments. Dr. Doe-Knocktay testified that her salary level reflected her consistency in obtaining merit awards based on her meritorious performance. Dr. Doe-Knocktay also noted that plaintiff has written several self-published books which include novels and opinion pieces, which contrasted to her own record of peer-reviewed publications and books published by university presses and other publishing houses. Dr. Doe-Knocktay also testified about plaintiff's interruption of faculty meetings and practice of writing memoranda with insulting remarks.

Doe-Knocktay earned a *doctorat de troisième cycle* in 1975 from the University of Paris Vll. She studied film and wrote as her thesis, "Le Concept du Noir comme Héros dans les films d'Expression Noire (1971-1973)." Doe-Knocktay stated categorically that her doctorate was the equivalent of the Ph.D in the United States.

Indeed, she affirms in her *curriculum vitae* that she earned the Ph.D. from the University of Paris Vll in 1975. The West Indian intellectual had drawn the attention of the court to the fact that in 1975 there were three levels of doctorates awarded by the University of Paris, the highest of which was the *doctorat d'état*.

The professional qualification earned by lawyers in the United States is a doctorate, a *juris doctor*. In the United States, physicians earn an M.D., a doctorate in medicine. In the British system, physicians do not earn doctorates. However, in the British system as in the United States, physicians are addressed by the title "Doctor." Doe-Knockktay confidently asserted that a doctorate is a doctorate. However, the lightly literate lawyer for the Capstone would never dream of attaching to himself the title "Doctor." Indeed, lawyers, as well as doctors, who wish to attain the highest levels of knowledge proceed from their professional doctorates to earn a Ph.D.

Contrary to Doe-Knocktay's sworn testimony, all doctorates are not created equal. In the United States, the Ph.D. is the mother of all doctorates. In the French system, the *doctorat d'état* was the mother of all doctorates. Subsequent to 1975, the French restructured their system so that they now have just one doctorate, the *doctorat unique*. There still are many different kinds of doctorates in the United States, even within the same discipline. For example, in the field of education, some candidates receive the Ed.D., and some, the Ph.D. Even in literary studies or the humanities, some receive the Ph.D., and some the D.A.

Doe-Knocktay's testimony did nothing to dispel the doubts raised about the equivalence of her *doctorat de toisième cycle* in film studies. Doe-Knocktay asserted in her testimony that she did not deem the West Indian intellectual's books to be germane to his discipline. Indeed, she censured him for writing about topics which were of popular interest rather than sticking to his "Hispanic studies." Doe-Knocktay also declared, with ill-concealed pride, that she had never read any of the West Indian intellectual's nine books. The lightly literate lawyer accurately echoed her sentiments when he referred to the West Indian intellectual's writings as "novels and opinion pieces."

It is wishful thinking on Doe-Knocktay's part to construe her testimony as harmful to the West Indian intellectual. Whereas Doe-Knocktay is prone to indulge in velleities, her partner, Doe-Deeay, has demonstrated a proclivity toward cold-blooded, calculating malice. She is the one who most probably masterminded the scheme to launch a scurrilous accusation against the West Indian intellectual. Unfortunately, this scheme is consistent with the practice of the Capstone, where contemptible behavior seems to have become the norm rather than the exception.

CHAPTER FIVE

The Affirmative Action Program v African Self-Affirmation

How long will they kill our prophets
While we stand one side and look?
BOB MARLEY

The West Indian intellectual, in word and deed, had called into question the Capstone's interpretation and implementation of the Affirmative Action Program in higher education. Such an outrage from a self-affirming foreign Black threatened the status quo, that is, the replacement of the ages-old affirmative action as white male privilege/entitlement by the HBCU style black American male privilege/entitlement. Such an uppity buck would have to be whipped into shape. The Capstone had worked for years to destroy the self-confidence of the West Indian intellectual, all to no avail. It decided, therefore, to contract the services of the ultimate "Negro-breaker," a twenty-first century version of Edward Covey of *The Life and Times of Frederick Douglass* (113).

The Capstone's coup de grace was to be the Expert Witness Report, and the expert witness was white, albeit just barely so, and male. He has the mien and the biography of a Sephardic Jew. But for his Hispanic antecedents he could easily be considered a very light-skinned Negro. The conscience of the Capstone of Negro education was, thus, somewhat mollified.

Expert Witnesses are not cheap. They can charge about five hundred dollars per hour. Money was no problem for the Capstone, however. It had the deepest of all possible pockets, the coffers of the federal government, filled to the brim and running over with taxpayers' dollars. So it did not hesitate to shell out ninety-five hundred dollars to the selected "hit man" to bring to his knees a self-confident West Indian intellectual who had dared to stand up like a man.

As the Office of the General Counsel of the Capstone was authorizing the generous payment to tear down one of the few tier-one scholars at the institution, the president was honoring four law school students who had written a friend-of-the-court brief in support of the University of Michigan Affirmative Action admissions policy. A report on this action is presented in an internet article on the website, *Black College Wire*, on March 3, 2003. According to this article, the Capstone's president declared that "race trumps diversity." He also affirmed that the Capstone was one of the few companies, organizations, or schools to emphasize race sensitivity. Kurt Schmoke, the dean of the Capstone's School of Law, joined his leader in asserting that "race-conscious measures are constitutionally admissible to avoid discrimination."

Schmoke had been a Rhodes scholar. Rhodes scholarships are one of the most fundamental vehicles for effecting affirmative action as white male privilege/entitlement. They are named after an arch-racist British strongman who was responsible for plundering untold billions of Africa's wealth during the nineteenth century. It is not surprising, then, that Schmoke would be inclined to interpret the Affirmative Action Program in higher education as the black American version of the traditional affirmative action as white privilege/entitlement. It is worthy of note that Alain Locke was also a Rhodes scholar.

Gwendolyn Majette, one of the faculty members of the Capstone's School of Law who directed the four valiant filers of the *amicus* brief, made a telling point. She is reported to have asserted that:

> The fact remains that the interpretations of the courts are based upon their own personal experiences . . . [The logic of whites] is not ours—as people of color we experience a different reality that shapes our interpretation [of reality]. Things that make sense to us don't always make sense to them, and the precedent of the legal system is what matters.

The president of the Capstone is a Howard trained lawyer. It is reasonable to conclude that Majette's opinion expressed in the preceding quote is shared by him and by the Office of the General Counsel of the Capstone.

Conscious of the fact that "things that make sense to us don't always make sense to them," that is, to white folks, the Capstone paid a white man (albeit barely so) the princely sum of ninety-five hundred dollars to assess the credentials of a faculty member who had declared himself to be Afrocentric. Naturally, things that made sense to the Afrocentric West Indian intellectual did not always make sense to the Eurocentric Expert Witness. This did not matter to the anointed leaders of the Capstone. All that mattered was the tearing down of a tier-one scholar who had not been anointed like them.

Like Locke, the Expert Witness is a Harvard man, but unlike Locke, he had risen to the pinnacle of the mainstream Eurocentric academic system, because he was the beneficiary of the affirmative action of white male privilege/entitlement, the bedrock of Western societies. Some Africans have found Whites from the Hispanic world to be more virulently affirmative of their self-declared supremacy than pure-blooded WASPs. And this is understandable, for after five hundred years of racial mixing there are probably no pure Aryans left in Latin America.

Undermining African Self-Confidence

The Expert Witness begins his Report with the declaration:

> I write at the request of [the lightly literate lawyer] on behalf of his client, Howard University, defendant in a suit brought against it by Professor Ian Isidore Smart. The suit alleges institutional discrimination on the basis of national origin and religion. It further alleges that, for discriminatory reasons, his salary is lower than it should be, that he has been unfairly passed over for administrative positions, and that such treatment by the University is incommensurate with his academic preeminence.
>
> My responsibility here is to render an opinion on whether or not the West Indian intellectual's claim to preeminence is justified.

Accused of systematic discrimination against the West Indian intellectual, the Capstone responds by paying a militantly Eurocentric scholar a princely sum of money to address the question of academic preeminence. Common sense should have indicated to the president of the Capstone (a lawyer himself) and his attorneys that the fundamental issue raised by the West Indian intellectual's suit is not academic preeminence, but unequal treatment. Whatever criteria were used at the Capstone to assess the merits of African American and other non-West Indian faculty should be used to assess the merits of the West Indian intellectual. There is no evidence that the Capstone used academic preeminence as a standard for assessing the merits of its faculty members during the twenty-five years of the West Indian intellectual's tenure at the institution.

The Expert Witness thus is hoisted on his own petard. He has missed the point, *bene cucurrit sed extra viam*. He comes along to set up super criteria which he claims are the standard for Academe. This claim is suspect, but the point is moot. The only standards that apply are those which were used at Howard University between 1997 and 2002 to award merit increases. These are the standards which permitted the University in one instance to award two merit increases to a new assistant professor of French, who does not have a Ph.D. from a department of French. Of course, this anointed assistant professor is an African American.

> *Professor Smart's Claims*: Professor Smart claims preeminence in Hispanic studies, in Afro-Hispanic literature, and in Carnival Studies. In the Interrogatory of 4 December 2002, he characterizes himself as "one of the leading Hispanists in the world" and as a scholar of "world-class reputation." Such self-regard seems to be characteristic of his own public opinion of himself: for instance, in his self-nomination for a Distinguished Service Award in 1996, he claims that he "provides his students the ultimate university experience, that of being taught by a world-class critic and literary figure as well." In the web pages advertising his books, most of them published in his own press, he claims, for instance, for one book that it is "impeccably well-written and compellingly documented," for another that it is a "brilliant act of signifying," for

> another that it is "innovative," for another that it is "valuable . . . [and] excellent," for yet another that it is "authoritative, challenging, and stimulating." In his "Plaintiff's Response to First Interrogatories," he describes his publishing record as consisting of "9 books and more than 60 [other] publications"; as having published, in 1996, "one of the most important books in Hispanic Studies" [this would be *Amazing Connections*]; and being a "scholar of world-class reputation" and "the only true scholar left in the Department." He believes "less qualified" faculty in his department have undeservedly higher salaries than he does.

The Expert Witness is setting up the West Indian intellectual's entire scholarly contribution for demolition by the old adage: "self-praise is no praise." This, of course, is an adage dear to good Negroes. In our society, however, only losers shy away from presenting themselves in the most positive light. The Expert Witness, steeped in Eurocentricism, automatically interprets self-confidence in a Black man as arrogance, positive self-representation as inordinate self-praise.

Maintaining African Underdevelopment

The report asserts:

> *Salary issues in general* : Salaries at universities are based on several criteria: promotions, cost-of-living increases (when awarded), merit increases, and—most tellingly—increases due to outside offers. At the full professor rank, these offers should come generally from universities better than one's own and/or at salaries better than one's present salary, offering working conditions better

> than one's present conditions. Aside from offers at the full professor rank, the most important evidence for preeminence in one's field would be offers of Endowed Chairs from other universities. Absent outside offers, especially at the Endowed Chair level, a faculty member would have great difficulty making credible claims for preeminence.
>
> Universities respond to market pressure. Without it, even well-respected professors who are not courted by other universities may earn salaries which are only average for the department and for time in rank.
>
> I am aware of no evidence that Professor Smart has received outside offers at the senior level.

The immediate response to the above from anyone who has had the slightest experience with the reality on the ground at HBCUs, even at the Capstone, would be: "What planet did the Expert Witness come from?" There is a joke which circulates in HBCU circles about a brilliant young faculty member who received an "outside offer." The young man, still wet behind the ears, went to the Negro college president confident that he would win at least a matching salary. The response of the Negro college president was: "Write us when you get there."

The West Indian intellectual, in the course of his twenty-five years at the Capstone, would from time to time grow exceedingly weary and would begin to look elsewhere. He would, however, eventually renew his optimism, especially under the inspiration of the example of faculty members such as Ron Walters. A few years ago the inevitable occurred: Walters moved to the University of Maryland College Park. Surely, when the offer from College Park came, Walters would have tried to play the game outlined by the Expert Witness. Surely, the president of the Capstone, a man who earned six hundred thousand dollars in 2001, must have reacted like the typical Negro college president.

Indeed, when the West Indian intellectual heard that Walters had been “raided” by College Park, he sent off a letter to the president of the Capstone chiding him for his dereliction of duty in having allowed the University’s most distinguished faculty member to be “raided” on his watch. As was only to be expected, the president of the Capstone did not dignify the West Indian intellectual’s letter with a response.

The only way the Capstone has managed to keep the lid on faculty discontent over the egregious disparities in the area of salaries is by concealing the data. Not aware of the strict code of silence, the Expert Witness spills all of the beans in his report.

> *Specific salaries at the DMLL [Department of Modern Languages and Literatures] (Howard University):* There are eight full professors in the DMLL. Professor Smart’s salary is currently $73,782. Above him in salary are Professors Bigger Thomas ($82,855) and Jane Doe-Knocktay ($86, 229). Below him are other full professors, and the lowest salary for a full professor in the DMLL is $59,518. Professor Smart’s salary, therefore, is the third highest in the department.

The names of the two favored colleagues have been fictionalized. Jane Doe-Knocktay is the same individual referenced in chapter 4 in the e-mail communication from a colleague identified as Jane Doe-Deeay. Doe-Knocktay is about the same age as the West Indian intellectual, who was born in 1944. Thomas is an African American male close to eighty years of age. To counter allegations made by the West Indian intellectual that Howard University had pursued a policy of systematic discrimination on the basis of national origin, the upper administration had in the course of five years increased Doe-Knocktay's salary by 35 percent. Thomas had been placed on the Affirmative Action gravy train from the earliest days. This explains his salary. The West Indian intellectual's salary above represents an increase of about seven thousand dollars (that is about 11 percent) over the five-year period.

This situation meets all of the specifications presented in the Willie Lynch speech at James River. The Negroes are thoroughly divided. Those who happen to have been born in the United States have been anointed. West Indian intellectuals have been a significant part of the academic foundation of the HBCUs. This is especially the case consequent on the ending of the Apartheid system in higher education and the siphoning off of the best African American minds to mainstream institutions. Howard University would cease to exist as an academic institution without the input of West Indian students and faculty. However, West Indians are still nothing more than foreign Blacks. A Black born in Europe is quite different. Such a person carries a European Union passport. Such a person can enter the United States almost at will. To get a visa to travel to "paradise," West Indians have to go through a humiliating scrutiny.

The authorities at the Capstone mistakenly assumed that all foreign born Blacks are equal. They saw Doe-Knocktay as counting for two credits, as a foreign Black and as a female. So they piled favors on her. They upped her salary twenty-two thousand dollars in five years. They proclaimed her the intellectual par excellence. She was loathe to accept all of these manifestly undeserved honors, but was happy for the monetary benefits.

The Expert Witness was born and raised in Latin America. He is Harvard trained and a literary scholar. He knows what's what. He must have smiled knowingly to himself, pocketed the ninety-five hundred dollars, and proceeded to tear down the reputation of the tier-one West Indian intellectual without too much hesitation. After all, it was a Negro thing. They were fighting among themselves as usual. Hispanics do it. Arabs do it. Asians from the Indian subcontinent do it. Everybody does it, it seems. So why should he have any qualms about taking money to aid and abet one of the many sides in this incessant internecine strife.

The Expert Witness makes a very creative argument to justify Thomas's income. He first presents the norms for the industry with regard to administrative positions:

> The main criteria for internal administrative appointments are: the ability to be effective on a personal level with faculty and administrators both below and above the position, in other words, to possess good interpersonal skills; the ability to handle budgets responsibly and to understand how to apportion resources effectively and fairly (especially important in eras of shrinking budgets); the ability to carry out an institutional vision and to place one's own professional or research agenda within the larger institutional agenda or be willing to put it to one side; the ability to deal with a variety of issues—some of which may be inflammatory or highly emotional—calmly, rationally, and effectively; the ability to deal with a wide range of demands and requests from individual faculty and administrators; the ability to represent the University to the wider world.

"The logic of whites is not ours." So the Expert Witness is not really to blame for his inability to make an effective analysis of the situation at the Capstone. He had, in effect, been set up by those who bought his services. He reasonably assumes that since Thomas had enjoyed a long career as an administrator at HBCUs that he must have met the criteria which are standard in the Academy.

The Expert Witness avers that the comparison between the

West Indian intellectual and Thomas is "largely irrelevant." "Professor Thomas came to Howard as an administrator, hired away from Texas Southern University." Texas Southern University is a historically black college, and Howard is the premiere HBCU. A move from being a chair at Texas Southern to mere faculty member status at Howard is a lateral move. The Expert Witness misses this point, and he is certainly ignorant of the fact that Thomas left the department at Texas Southern in shambles.

"At Howard, he [Thomas] served as associate department chair, as department chair (twice) and for eight years as associate dean of the Graduate School." The details are correct, however the chronology has been inverted. Moreover, the West Indian intellectual, having come to the Department in the same year as Thomas, knows from firsthand observation that this latter was "associate chair" of the Department of Romance Languages in name only. The title had been given to him by a kindly elderly lady who served as chair. After hanging around the department for two or three years as make-belief "associate chair," Thomas was appointed by the central administration of the Capstone to a real position as associate dean in the Graduate School. As is the custom at the Capstone, this was more of an anointment than an appointment. There was no realistic search process, no competition for the post.

Thomas served for eight years in the Graduate School. At the end of this period *he was demoted* to the chairmanship of the Department of Romance Languages. And this move was also effected through administrative fiat. Indeed, there had been a search for the post of chair of the Department. The candidate who won the majority of the votes was the incumbent, Keith Warner. However, just one week before he was due to begin his third term, he was summarily relieved of his post so that Thomas could occupy it, even though Thomas had not been one of the candidates for the position.

The faculty were bitterly opposed to Thomas's chairmanship, but not having the courage to take an open stand, they turned to the West Indian intellectual. He had been a candidate for the position and had received only a small minority of the votes. He, therefore, advised his colleagues to seek the help of the one in whom they had put their trust by giving him the majority of their votes. Thomas proved to be a most inept chair, and since the intense opposition of the faculty did not diminish, he was removed from office after his first term.

The logic of whites (which must be assumed to be consonant with the logic of the Expert Witness) is certainly not the logic of the central administration at the Capstone. After a dismal performance and dismissal from the chairmanship, Thomas was inexplicably called out of the shadows to take a crack at running and ruining the Department once more, this time as interim chair. This second time, Thomas only lasted one year before he was again sent back to the shadows.

Thomas has been the most hated and the most incompetent person to chair the Department in the twenty-five years in which the West Indian intellectual has served. This view will be corroborated by a majority of the faculty who experienced his "leadership." Perhaps the Expert Witness suspected that there was something amiss with Thomas's record, for he comments with what might be calculated irony: "Given his age, his many years of service and his leadership at Howard, I would ask not why his salary is higher than Professor Smart's but why his salary is not higher than $82,855."

Discrediting African Self-Publishing

The Expert Witness, sensing that freedom of the press is only guaranteed to those who own one, is most troubled by the West Indian intellectual's self-affirmation through ownership of a press. White supremacy can be justified only if the truth about the African origin of civilization is suppressed. Freedom of the press is utterly incompatible with the suppression of this fundamental information. Through his publishing activities the West Indian intellectual has sought to empower Africans with the truth about their history. The Expert Witness, a white-looking Latin American Harvard man, has benefitted fully from the program of affirmative action as white male privilege/entitlement, one of the foundations of Western civilization. He must, then, out of self-preservation, seek to discredit utterly the West Indian intellectual's self-affirmation through ownership of a press, for if this were allowed to develop, it could lead to the empowerment of a critical mass of Afrocentric intellectuals.

Many have been the pious publications proffered by the antislavery lobby of the Eurocentric Academy. In the first chapter of this book, reference was made to one such work by Henri Grégoire, the English translation of which was published in Brooklyn in 1810. The title is quaintly direct: *An Enquiry Concerning the Intellectual and Moral Faculties and Literature of Negroes: Followed with an Account of the Life and Works of Fifteen Negroes and Mulattoes Distinguished in Science, Literature and the Arts.* One of the exceptional Negroes studied in the work was Francis Williams, who was born at the turn of the eighteenth century. It was in this same eighteenth century that Count Constantin François de Chassebœuf de Volney wrote his much quoted lines:

> There [in "Black Africa"] a people, now forgotten, discovered, while others were yet barbarians, the elements of the arts and sciences. A race of men now rejected from society for their *sable skin and frizzled hair*, founded on the study of the laws of nature, those civil and religious systems which still govern the universe. (Quoted in *Amazing Connections* 13)

However, Thomas Jefferson, considered by the mainstream Academy to be a moderate and a champion of liberty and justice, was clearly not persuaded by the arguments of Grégoire, Volney, and the plethora of benevolent white scholars. Jefferson had no problem consigning Africans to the status of three-fifths human. The only publications which can effect the liberation from mental and physical slavery are the self-publications of Africans and other nonwhite peoples. The Expert Witness, in his heart of hearts, is aware of this reality. It is for this reason that the Expert Witness is so resolutely opposed to the West Indian intellectual's self-publications.

The core of the Expert Witness Report is contained in the following paragraph:

> Of Professor Smart's first three books, two went through the peer review process. . . . The third book, *Short Stories by Cubena*, was published by the Afro-Hispanic Institute, which Professor Smart co-founded and helped to administer. The fourth through the ninth book (from *Pastrana's Last River* to *Spoiled Priest*) were all published either by the Afro-Hispanic Institute or by the Original World Press, which Professor Smart founded in 1994. One of these publications can be considered a "service" publication: the translation, and thus dissemination, of *El ultimo río* or *Pastrana's Last River* by the Ecuadorian writer Nelson Estupiñán Bass. The remainder can be considered either as 'vanity publications' or as

> 'unjuried publications' whose quality was not attested to, prior to publication, by the peer review process. Therefore of his nine books, only two were professionally juried. . . . The modest and lukewarm reception concerning most of his works is not what one would expect for, in Professor Smart's words, "one of the leading Hispanists in the world."

The Expert Witness does deserve, after all, every one of those nine thousand five hundred dollars (U.S. currency) paid him by the Capstone. He appears to have administered a sound whipping to the uppity foreign Black. He had been retained precisely for this purpose, fulfilling a function analogous to that of Edward Covey in Frederick Douglass's world. Chapter 3 of this current book presented a true and complete account of the West Indian intellectual's publishing activity, and the reader is invited to compare this account to the Expert Witness's representation of it. The Expert Witness accepts as valid only those peer review processes over which the mainstream Eurocentric Academy exercises total control. Clearly, the leadership of the Capstone concurs with him in this.

The Expert Witness asserts further:

> The West Indian intellectual's is not the cv of one of the world's eminent Hispanists. He does have some standing in Afro-Hispanic literature, through his early publications, through his work for the Afro-Hispanic Institute and the *Afro-Hispanic Review*, and through conference participation, but in my view he does not have world preeminence in this field. As far as I can determine, his theories on the Kemetic/Egyptian influences on Afro-Hispanic literature have been largely ignored, due perhaps to the publication venue (Original World Press) or due to their questionable viability. More serious attention might have been given his views if he had been able to publish *Amazing Connections* with, say, Rutgers University Press,

> which published Martin Bernal's *Black Athena: The Afroasiatic Roots of Classical Civilization*. He might then have become a voice in the ongoing dialogues and controversies concerning this important subject.

In the Expert Witness's mind there exists the mainstream Academy with its uncompromisingly Eurocentric focus and then some other minority voices, which can be permitted to operate under careful supervision. The record shows that in 1993 the manuscript of *Amazing Connections* was juried by the University of Missouri Press. The reader recommended publication by a "commercial" press precisely because of its controversial nature. Martin Bernal is a British scholar of Semitic origin. He was trained at the School of Oriental Studies of London University and was given a teaching position at Cambridge University. Consistent with the process outlined earlier on in the Expert Witness Report, which is standard for the mainstream Eurocentric Academy, Bernal was picked up by the Department of Government Studies of Cornell. There he was given a long period of study leave, without any teaching assignments, in order to devote himself exclusively to his work on *Black Athena*.

There is credible evidence that Bernal was chosen to be "the great white hope" in the field of Afrocentric studies. Although he was a Cornell professor, his book (two volumes so far) has been published by Rutgers University Press. Ivan Van Sertima, who is deemed by Afrocentric scholars to be the informal dean of their discipline, teaches at Rutgers University. However, Van Sertima's major book, *They Came Before Columbus: The African Presence in Ancient America,* was not published by Rutgers University Press, but rather by Random House, a commercial press. Van Sertima's work challenges the assumptions on which white supremacy rests. There is no way it would be published by a university press. Indeed, even after the great success of *They Came Before Columbus*, the Rutgers University professor has not had any of his books published by his home university press.

Van Sertima has taken the route of self-affirmation through ownership of a press. He founded Transaction Press in order to give voice not only to his work, but to that of an entire generation of Afrocentric scholars. Even after his outstanding success in Academe, Van Sertima was not promoted to full professor by Rutgers University. Van Sertima was born in Guyana, as was George G. M. James. Both of these scholars have been models for the West Indian intellectual.

It is worthy of note that when Cornell University employed Bernal in their Department of Government Studies they allowed him an extended period of freedom to pursue his investigations with all manner of assistance (which he acknowledges in the preface to the first volume of his work). When, in 1993, the West Indian intellectual began the study of Egyptian hieroglyphs, the Capstone did absolutely nothing to facilitate his work.

One of the Expert Witness's more cunning attacks on the West Indian intellectual's self-publishing is his apparently objective assessment of Gordon Rohlehr's review of *Amazing Connections*. Rohlehr's piece is described as: "Mostly a neutral and balanced review." For all his Harvard training the Expert Witness evinces a lack of familiarity with the spirit of understatement and self-effacement which pervades British academic culture. This spirit stands in marked contrast to the brash self-affirmation which has become the hallmark of everything American, even the academic culture.

In the United States students feel entitled to a grade of A, which is the equivalent of a score of 90 percent or higher. In the

British/Irish system—at least during the period in which the West Indian intellectual was a student—33 percent was the lowest passing score. Only the genuine geniuses could hope to attain a score of 75 percent or higher. Rohlehr was born in Guyana in 1942. He was trained in and never abandoned the system in which reticence, understatement, and self-effacement are cherished qualities. In such a system, Rohlehr's review of *Amazing Connections* would be seen as a very positive one. Even the Expert Witness has to acknowledge that the review "Ends positively."

Most importantly, the Expert Witness fails to take into account that Rohlehr is the master self-publisher. He formally rejected the "plantation press" in 1981 when—consistent with the Willie Lynch policy—it sought to drive a wedge between himself and Edward Kamau Brathwaite, two of the leading West Indian intellectuals of the twentieth century. If the Expert Witness had taken the trouble to look at a copy of Rohlehr's *Pathfinder: Black Awakening in* The Arrivants *of Edward Kamau Brathwaite,* he would have seen that the publisher is none other than Gordon Rohlehr.

The merciless assault narrows down to Carnival, and with the arrogance which characterizes the white supremacist, the Expert Witness presumes superiority over the West Indian intellectual in this field. The Expert Witness could not know much about Carnival. He is not aware that Rohlehr is the world's leading expert on the Trinidad and Tobago kaiso (calypso) and, as such, might be deemed to be "unavoidable"in any discussion of Carnival. Hopefully, one day the Expert Witness will get a chance to read Rohlehr's *Calypso & Society in Pre-Independence Trinidad.* This book was published in 1990, and the publisher is none other than Gordon Rohlehr.

The Expert Witness, carried away with his mandate, pontificates:

> His work on "carnival" (which has received some attention in Trinidad and Tobago) has not been taken up in academic journals or books, in the United States or elsewhere. . . .
>
> Carnival studies may be considered an area of specialization but it is not an academic field at this time. For instance, I am not aware of there being tenure-track lines in it, as there are in Afro-Hispanic Studies, or in Latin American Studies. In Carnival Studies, there are others who come to mind before Professor Smart: Mikhail Bakhtin, the brilliant Russian scholar and theorist (d. 1975) who is unavoidable in the field and yet does not appear in either the index or bibliography of *Ah Come Back Home*; Milla C. Riggio, who guest-edited a special issue of the *Drama Review* (1998) on "Trinidad and Tobago Carnival"; now Gerard Aching (because he published with a major academic press); and the older theatre scholar Errol Hill (whose *Trinidad Carnival: Mandate for a National Theatre*,1972, is a standard work).

When, in 1975, the West Indian intellectual completed his Ph.D. in Spanish at UCLA with a dissertation: "The Creative Dialogue in the Poetry of Nicolás Guillén: Europe and Africa," Afro-Hispanic studies was not considered an area of specialization. Even as late as the 1980s, Louis Hemans, another West Indian intellectual associated with the Capstone, was told by the leadership of the Department of Spanish and Portuguese of the University of Maryland, College Park that there was no such field as Afro-Hispanic Literature. The West Indian intellectual was one of the pioneers whose work contributed to the establishment of Afro-Hispanic Studies as "an academic field."

As a direct consequence of the publication of *Ah Come Back Home*, the West Indian intellectual was invited to a major conference on Carnival hosted by the Colombian Ministry of Education and the Barranquilla Carnival Foundation. Patricia Alleyne-Dettmers, a recognized scholar in the field of Carnival Studies (contrary to the view of the Expert Witness, Carnival Studies has already become an academic field—the Academy is developing at a much faster pace than the Expert Witness realizes) and a professor at the University of Hamburg, was also invited to the conference, solely on the basis of her participation in *Ah Come Back Home*. There was a total of twenty-three experts on Carnival from Europe, Latin America, and the Caribbean who were invited to the conference.

Mikhail Bakhtin, for all his brilliance, failed to understand the Kemetic roots of Carnival. The West Indian intellectual knows his work and does not consider it "unavoidable in the field." The Expert Witness got carried away with the Edward Covey role which the leadership of the Capstone had paid him so handsomely to play. He inadvertently adopts a relationship of superior to subaltern with respect to the West Indian intellectual. His self-confidence flows from the affirmative action as white male privilege/entitlement from which he has benefitted all of his life. The leadership of the Capstone was not fazed by this circumstance, for it would be consistent with an endorsement of the traditional white supremacist affirmative action.

Milla Riggio has done some important work. However, Riggio, a true scholar, will concede that the West Indian intellectual and his group have advanced the interests of Carnival Studies with their contribution. Riggio did invite the West Indian intellectual to contribute to her special edition of the *Drama Review*. However, since Riggio's approach is more Eurocentric than Afrocentric, the West Indian intellectual opted to withdraw his essay, using it rather as the basis of one of his contributions to*Ah Come Back Home*.

The Expert Witness admits that he recognizes the work of Gerard Aching (a Trinidadian professor of Spanish who currently teaches at NYU) solely because it was published by a major academic press. However, major academic presses do not publish Afrocentric scholarship. Earlier in his report the Expert Witness had established Aching's work as a determiner of academic worth when he asserted:

> For example, *Ah Come Back Home*, Professor Smart's other work, and the work of all his contributors are completely ignored by Gerard Aching in his recent book, *Masking and Power: Carnival and Popular Culture in the Caribbean* (University of Minnesota Press, 2002).

The circularity in the Expert Witness's reasoning is not untypical of Eurocentric academicians. The publication process is a cumbersome one, fraught with delays and disappointments. The West Indian intellectual completed his Ph.D. dissertation on Nicolás Guillén in 1975. He completed the manuscript of his book on Guillén some ten years later. The manuscript was accepted for publication in 1988. Guillén died in 1989, and the page proofs had to be amended. The book did not get to the shelves until late in 1990. The rule of thumb is that there exists a ten-year gap between publication of a book and the research on which it is based.

Indeed, Aching began working on his Carnival book in the early 1990s. When *Ah Come Back Home* appeared in print, the publication process for Aching's book was already at an advanced stage. The editors at the University of Minnesota Press would have had to make the call as to whether or not they would disrupt the flow of the publication process in order to include reference to the pioneering text on Carnival. They obviously decided against any disruption. It was a judgement made on the basis of financial and administrative considerations. It had nothing to do with academic worth.

The Expert Witness is supposedly committed to the truth, the whole truth, and nothing but the truth. But the Expert Witness was paid ninety-five hundred dollars by lawyers representing the Capstone. It was not in the interest of his principals to reveal the whole truth about Aching's failure to include mention of *Ah Come Back Home* in his book on Carnival.

As the Expert Witness is undoubtedly aware, not all university presses are created equal. Donald Herdeck was the chief cook and bottle washer at Three Continents Press, a publishing enterprise which the Expert Witness deems to be acceptable. Herdeck is a white male from the United States, and he took the West Indian intellectual under his wing in a relationship of master to apprentice. The young scholar and future chief cook and bottle washer of Original World Press as well as the Afro-Hispanic Institute Press gleaned invaluable experience and insight from this relationship. He learned, for example, that in the 1970s and early 1980s Herdeck's Three Continents Press published about five times as many books per year as did Howard University Press.

The West Indian intellectual is, hence, much more versed in the nuts and bolts of publishing than is the Expert Witness, his fat fees notwithstanding.

Invoking White Supremacy

The Expert Witness wraps up his Report as follows:

> Professor Smart's scholarship is rather uneven. Some of it is

good. Much of it is repetitive, and some of it is even cobbled together from previous publications to such an extent that many 'new' publications are not as new as they first appear. Much of the later work arises from an obsession with establishing Kemetic/Egyptian cultures as THE source of Caribbean and Pan-African practices. The fundamentally ideological nature and polemical tone of this later work may account, in part, for its lack of impact, as may its self-published status.

In sum, I do not find the evidence to support the Professor Smart's claims of preeminence in Hispanic Studies, Afro-Hispanic Studies, and Carnival Studies.

"Ooh! That hurt!" The Expert Witness is a very respectable academician. He could not be very proud of his Report, but he, too, must eat. The leadership at the Capstone spends taxpayers' dollars with consummate ease. Thus they did not stop to think that in mainstream Academe, scholarly reviews are a matter of courtesy. Lawyers are notoriously unfamiliar with the ways of Academe, and apparently the president of the Capstone is more of a lawyer than a university president. A report by a highly paid expert witness is of scant value among academicians of the mainstream. The report under consideration proved to be very useful to the West Indian intellectual, however, providing him with a framework around which he could construct his response to the Capstone's preposterous claims. He is very appreciative of this favor done him, albeit *per accidens*.

In a small book, *Sartre, los intelectuales y la política,* reporting on a series of discussions with the legendary Jean-Paul Sartre, the editors attribute the following to the Frenchman:

> El profesor de facultad es casi siempre—y lo era también en mi tiempo—un señor que ha hecho una tesis y que la repite durante to-

> da su vida.(52)
> [A university professor is almost always—and the same was the case in my time—a man who had written a thesis and spends the rest of his life defending it.]

The typical university professor, according to the foremost existentialist philosopher of the twentieth century, is an individual whose repetitiveness is a defining characteristic. How can one be too repetitive about the "African Origin of Civilization"? There is enough to say on this topic to take up one thousand lifetimes.

Doe-Knocktay clearly meets the definition of the university professor proposed by her countryman. She wrote a doctoral thesis on Blacks in the United States cinema. She went on to write a decade later a book in two parts on Blacks in African cinema. Then, plumbing the depths of derivative scholarship, she wrote a book length report on some conversations with a novelist friend, Maryse Condé. Neither Doe-Knocktay nor the lightly literate lawyer stopped to think that they had relegated the West Indian intellectual's "novels and opinion pieces" to the margins of Academe. Furthermore, Doe-Knocktay double-dipped at this trough as well, once in French and once in English.

Even as the Capstone and its minions laid out traps for the West Indian intellectual, they found themselves ensnared by their own devices. Doe-Knocktay revealed in the course of her deposition testimony a fundamental misunderstanding of what translation entails. Yet she proudly proclaims that she earned an award in 1995 for the translation into English of the original 1993 book-length report in French on her conversations with her novelist friend.

Doe-Knocktay declared that she was responsible for the "translation" of the text, but that Doe-Deeay was the one who rendered it into grammatical English. "Translation" for Doe-

Knocktay is merely providing the word for word correspondence between the French and English. This is precisely what is entailed in "machine translations." According to Doe-Knocktay's logic, anyone who writes English could enter material in a foreign language into a translation machine, correct the inevitable gaffs, and then claim that he was responsible for the "translation."

Sartre continues:

> Es además alguien que posee un poder al que está atado ferozmente: el de imponer a la gente, en nombre de un saber que ha acumulado, sus propias ideas, sin que los que lo escuchan tengan el derecho de discutirlas. . . .
>
> La única manera de aprender es discutir. Es también la única manera de volverse un hombre. Un hombre no es nada si no es un ser que duda. Pero también debe ser fiel a alguna cosa. Un intelectual, para mí, es esto: alguien que es fiel a una realidad política y social, pero que no deja de ponerla en duda. (52,54)
> [He is furthermore a person who holds a power to which he is fiercely attached: that of imposing on people, in the name of the knowledge he has acquired, his own ideas, without giving his students the right to discuss them. . . .
>
> The only way to learn is through discussion. It is also the only way to become a man. A man is not a man unless he knows how to question. But he must also be faithful to some ideology. This is what an intellectual is, in my view: someone who believes in a particular political and social ideology, but who ceaselessly questions it.]

By declaring him "ideological" and "polemical" the Expert Witness is offering the highest praise to the West Indian intellectual. However, in the interest of pleasing his principals, he represents intellectual excellence as exactly its opposite. And he seems to think that his training and experience entitle him to make authoritative pronouncements about Afrocentric scholarship. He certainly has completely hoodwinked the lightly literate lawyer, for whom "ideological" and "polemical" translate into "opinion pieces."

The Hiphop artiste (Hiphoppa), KRS-ONE, in his book *Ruminations* (published in 2003), presents a position on "mis-education" (a idea made famous by Carter G. Woodson in his classic, *The Mis-Education of the Negro*) which echoes the Satrean view. The Socratic maxim that the unexamined life is not worth living was, in fact, adduced by the Hiphoppa in his presentation of what he labels "Urban Inspirational Metaphysics" and is reformulated later on in the book as follows:

> By questioning reality, you are made intelligent, and by way of intelligence, you can question reality. Presently, however, in many public and private schools people are taught questions and answers at the same time and at a very young age. (250)

The approach of teaching questions and answers at the same time certainly has its place, the inculcation of religious dogma. Thus the time-honored text known as the *Baltimore Catechism* was precisely a little book of questions and answers which little boys and girls committed to memory, usually under the strict supervision of nuns. KRS-ONE exposes the fact that

> . . . in today's education, it is more important to get an A, B, or C grade than it is to actually have the truth. This is the general scheme of education in America. Questioning what you have memorized is not required to pass your class. (250)

As far as the Hiphoppa is concerned, the *Baltimore Catechism* approach has become the norm.

It is particularly instructive that a former dean of the College of Arts and Sciences at the Capstone, in the course of his deposition testimony, arrogated to himself the right to censure the West Indian intellectual's teaching style. The haughty former dean boasted that in his parasitology course of thirty-five students only two were "given" a grade of A. He is thus representative of the dysfunctional approach to scholarship flagged by KRS-ONE.

> Therefore, you can go through most of your entire education life without critically thinking at all. All you have to do is memorize the teachings before you, even if it isn't necessarily the truth. This is called training. This sort of education keeps us on a primitive animalistic level. . . .
>
> . . . . In this case you are not an intellectual, you are a Memorex tape. . . .
>
> . . . . By doubting and questioning, you are given movement of thought. By accepting, you are chained down in thought, and chained down in life. (250-52)

The West Indian intellectual has consistently adopted an approach which conforms completely with the following KRS-ONE declarations:

> I cannot stress enough how important it is for you to be an independent thinker. Do not look for others to help you; help yourself, even if you have to move away from your present environment. . . . Only your mental strength can help control your life. . . .
>
> . . . . Anyone who educates you controls your speech. . . .
>
> . . . . The true Hiphoppa understands why freedom of speech is

not as important as freedom of thought. (254-55)

Lyndon B. LaRouche, the most consistent candidate for the presidency of the United States, within hours of the September 11, 2001 events, suggested that it was an "inside job." The Bush administration and, indeed, most of humanity bristled at the horrendous implications of LaRouche's allegation. However, consequent on the Machiavellian manipulation of the tragedy by the Bush administration, the suggestion does not now seem so far-fetched to most of humanity. For, indeed, the Bush administration has reaped windfall profits from Nine-One-One. They have used it to justify the devastation of Afghanistan from the relative safety of the air. Then they moved in without too much problem to occupy the areas needed to construct the pipeline on which they had set their hearts.

They had also set their hearts on controlling the oil of Iraq. However, the perpetrators of Nine-One-One could not be connected to Iraq in any way. So a connection had to be fabricated. Martin Bernal, in the introduction to the first volume of *Black Athena* reveals the truth about "The Fabrication of Ancient Greece." This is the label he gives to the process by which scholars of the Enlightenment recreated the history of civilization to suit their ideological preferences.

For all of the history of mankind, it had been accepted that the Greeks knew what they were talking about when they claimed that their civilization came from Egypt. This truth was disturbing to European scholars at the end of eighteenth century, for Egypt is part of Africa, and the systematic pillaging of Africa had fabulously enriched Europe. If the ancients and some of the honest contemporary scholars (such as Volney) were right, then the trans-Atlantic slave trade and the enslavement of Africans would indeed constitute the most horrendous of crimes against humanity. A new history clearly needed to be fabricated. And the Aryan Model was created to replace the Ancient Model. According to the new logic, Greek civilization developed from an incursion from the north, it was an Aryan civilization.

Since the Aryan Model flew in the face of all the data, it was impossible to construct plausible explanations for all of the observable phenomena. There are huge logical gaps. For example, the theorem named after Pythagoras is known to have been explained in a papyrus from one of the Kemetic institutions of higher learning. This papyrus is dated to 2000 B.C., whereas Pythagoras was born some 1400 years later. It is generally accepted by the Eurocentric Academy that philosophical speculation was invented by the pre-Socratic Greeks of the sixth century B.C. However, there abound philosophical texts from Kemet which can be dated at least to the third millennium B.C.

The process by which the idea of Western civilization was generated is one in which conclusions that are per se preposterous can be made to appear reasonable. As a result of this kind of process, 600 B.C. predates 2000 B.C. Since the idea of Western civilization is based on a network of fabrications, it was easy for the Bush administration to palm off the fabrications about Iraq's involvement in Nine-One-One. The overall reasoning of the Expert Witness is a good example of the process by which conclusions which are preposterous per se can be presented cleverly to appear reasonable. In the case of the Expert Witness's assessment of the relative contributions of the West Indian intellectual, Professor Doe-Knocktay, and Professor Thomas, the conclusion reached is that 177 is greater than 277, and that 63 is also greater than 277.

In evaluating the qualifications of faculty members it is convenient to award ten points for a published book, five points for a refereed article, etc. On this scale it would be reasonable to award ten points for founding a journal or a press or for creating a website. In the specific cases under consideration, there are anomalies in the matter of the entry level qualifications, so there had to be some readjustments. The West Indian intellectual earned a Ph.D. in Spanish and was awarded ten points. Professor Thomas earned a Ph.D. in foreign language education, but has the title of professor of French. He was awarded just seven points.

Professor Doe-Knocktay in 1975 earned a *doctorat de troisième cycle* in film studies from the University of Paris VII. Her declarations notwithstanding, this simply does not equate to the Ph.D. in French, the normal entry-level requirement for the rank of assistant professor of French. In her case, as in Thomas's, the Capstone made an exception. Objectively, however, her doctorate, like Thomas's, would be awarded only seven points.

The Expert Witness made every attempt to appear logical in his evaluation. The West Indian intellectual had nine published books, Thomas had none, and Doe-Knocktay had four (actually, two, in two parts each). The Expert Witness, by virtue of the authority invested in him as a Harvard man, determined that only two of the West Indian intellectual's books really counted. Invoking the same authority, he counted as publications two of Doe-Knocktay's manuscripts which were still forthcoming.

In the business of academic publishing there is many a slip between the cup and the lip. There is one notorious case in the Department of a faculty member who, to secure his promotion to associate professor as well as to full professor, used the page proofs of a book which was never going to be published. In the recent past, some faculty members in the department have been promoted to the rank of full professor on the basis of books which existed only as bibliographical references. Of course, this does not present any particular problem at the Capstone, where administrators and colleagues alike have proudly proclaimed that they had not read a single one of the West Indian intellectual's books.

The West Indian intellectual's credentials are at least equal to those of the Expert Witness, and by virtue of the power vested in him as a full professor of Spanish, he has determined that all nine of his books are to be counted. The Capstone, then, has to decide whose word it will accept, that of the Afrocentric West Indian intellectual or that of the Eurocentric Expert Witness.

There are some scholars held in high esteem by the mainstream Academy who have declared the plural of "magnum opus" to be "*magni opi*." The Expert Witness might be cut from the same sciolistic cloth as these colleagues. It might be useful for the Capstone in weighing the respective credentials of the West Indian intellectual and the Expert Witness to have the two confront each other in a free-style. It would be "meet and just" to have this contest based exclusively on the scholars' knowledge of Latin and Middle Egyptian.

CHAPTER SIX

Emancipating Ourselves from Mental Slavery

Hereditary bondmen, know ye not
Who would be free, themselves must strike the blow?
LIFE AND TIMES OF FREDERICK DOUGLASS

Shortly after his grand installation, a veritable pseudo-coronation, the current president proclaimed as the Capstone's defining slogan: "Leadership for America and the Global Community." The current dean of the Capstone's Graduate School of Arts and Sciences has enthusiastically inaugurated a campaign to take the graduate program to "tier-one status." James E. Cheek, who presided over the Capstone for two decades and had at one time considered himself president-for-life, would proudly proclaim that Howard belonged to the same class of institutions as Duke, Yale, Harvard, etc. He clearly believed that the premiere HBCU (Historically Black College or University) had already achieved tier-one status and was already exercising leadership for America and the global community. Cheek was ousted by the students in a 1989 revolt.

The leadership at the Capstone has charted its course to success through its interpretation of the Affirmative Action

Program in higher education. It appears to have failed to understand that the most effective form of Affirmative Action is the self-affirmation enjoined in Marcus Garvey's dictum, do for self. Its failure to comprehend this truth is only to be expected, for the evidence suggests that the leadership was itself appointed not on merit, but through the program of African American privilege which prevails in HBCUs and which, at times, even trumps the affirmative action as white privilege/entitlement.

The Capstone and the other HBCUs were created by the federal government of the United States to train Negroes to fit harmoniously into mainstream civil society. However, this mainstream civil society was fundamentally white supremacist, based squarely on the system of affirmative action as white male privilege/entitlement. The Affirmative Action Program which was developed as a consequence of the Civil Rights movement is purported to have as its ultimate goal the dismantling of the old affirmative action as white male privilege. Few and far between are the intellectuals who understand the relationship between the two mutually exclusive forms of affirmative action. West Indian intellectuals, because of their peculiar experience with the British colonial educational system, have tended to understand the relationship.

It follows, then, that West Indian intellectuals have a key role to play in helping HBCU communities make the most effective use of the Affirmative Action Program in higher education. In these times of economic hardship, the entire Affirmative Action concept is under attack, and the Program will most likely be scrapped or significantly reduced in scope. It is an open secret that the HBCUs serve as mere tokens of white supremacy's crocodile contrition for its past and present assaults on the selfhood of nonwhite Americans. However, the damage done to the self-concept of nonwhites can only be repaired through their self-determination. The Capstone and the other HBCUs, then, must reassess their approach to the Affirmative Action Program not only to keep it alive as a symbol, but to secure real benefits from it. Since those forces which seek to end the Affirmative Action Program would also close down the HBCUs, adaptation to the prevailing reality is a matter of life or death for HBCUs as much as for the Program.

It is in the salary structure that the Capstone manifests most glaringly its adherence to the perverted interpretation of the Affirmative Action Program. In defending itself against the allegations of the West Indian intellectual, the Capstone engaged the services of a highly paid Expert Witness. The latter, in the course of his Report, presented what he judged to be the norm in mainstream Eurocentric Academe with respect to salaries. As previously cited, he avers:

> Salaries at universities are based on several criteria: promotions, cost-of-living increases (when awarded), merit increases, and—most tellingly—increases due to outside offers. At the full professor rank, these offers should come generally from universities better than one's own and/or at salaries better than one's present salary, offering working conditions better than one's present conditions....
>
> Universities respond to market pressure. Without it, even well-respected professors who are not courted by other universities may earn salaries which are only average for the department and for time in rank.

The situation outlined above is, in fact, the norm for the Academy. It is based ultimately on merit and on the checks and balances of the free market.

Salaries at the Capstone, on the other hand, appear to be based solely on the perverted interpretation of the Affirmative Action Program in higher education. The West Indian intellectual is one of several faculty members who made repeated requests to the current president of the Capstone for a presentation of the criteria established by his administration for assessing requests for merit awards. The merit award system was introduced by this president in 1997, and as of the writing of this book, no clear delineation of the criteria has ever been presented to the Capstone's faculty and staff. The national press, however, reported that this president essentially awarded himself a merit increase of over fifty percent in 2001. This brought his annual salary for 2001 to six hundred thousand dollars.

In such a corrupt system secrecy must be maintained. Fortunately, the Expert Witness, not being aware of the level of corruption at the Capstone, broke the code of silence in his Report. He disclosed that in the Department of Modern Languages and Literatures at the Capstone, as of July 1, 2002, the three highest salaries at the full professor rank were $73,782, $82,855, and $86, 229. The lowest salary for a full professor in the Department was $59,518. Since the president's 2001 salary of six hundred thousand dollars represented a 54 percent increase over his 2000 salary, it is likely that by the time this present book is published his income may be closer to the million dollar mark.

Only a tiny minority of the faculty and staff of the Capstone have been granted tickets to ride the Affirmative Action gravy train. There is consequently considerable restlessness among the "natives" at the Capstone. The West Indian intellectual, after more than two decades of trying to reason with the upper administration—a tiny group of privileged African Americans—took the expensive step of filing a lawsuit. This action may trigger a wave of litigation against the Capstone. The fact is that the so-called "merit" award system implemented by the current president of the Capstone is calculated to frustrate the self-affirmation of all but a tiny group of anointed African Americans. It thus frustrates the progress of the vast majority of African Americans and all other Africans towards liberating themselves from mental slavery.

Finding a Way Forward

In 1992, the Capstone obtained a grant from the National Endowment for the Humanities (NEH) to devise a humanities program which would fit the needs of an HBCU. The result was a two-course series, an "Introduction to the Humanities," having as its catchy logo the expression "Broad Sympathy" culled from the writings of W. E. B. DuBois, who was, until he attained middle age, merely another light-skinned, Harvard-trained Negro. The "Course Study Guide & Syllabus," produced by the group of Howard humanists funded by the NEH, is based on a militantly Eurocentric model. It declares:

> Historically in the Academy, the notion of the *humanities* derives from the *humanists* of the Italian and English Renaissance, who reacted to the heavy emphasis which the medieval educational system placed on philosophy (and especially logic) by reemphasizing the centrality of the *litterae humaniores*, or classical literature, history, and moral philosophy to their educational system and world view. (2)

Mercer Cook, mentioned by name in the document, is listed as one of the great Howard humanists. Indeed, the West Indian intellectual was part of the group funded by the NEH. However, Cook's work on Diop was virtually ignored, as were the interventions of the West Indian intellectual, during the deliberations at the Capstone that summer.

The document shows that the Howard University humanists understood the importance of studying the past in order to construct workable programs for the contemporary period. They deemed this "past" to be only those periods certified by Eurocentrism to be of value. Such periods bear the stamp "classical." The West Indian intellectual and all scholars in the Afrocentric school also study the past in order to better understand the present and to prepare adequately for the future. The West Indian intellectual and his co-editor, Kimani Nehusi (another West Indian intellectual), for example, adopted precisely this approach in *Ah Come Back Home: Perspectives on the Trinidad and Tobago Carnival*. If the people who created Carnival are to regain control of their festival, they must understand its origins.

Most of the criticism of progressive thinkers comes from those mired in the paralysis and unoriginality of the dogmatic *magister-dixit* approach to scholarship. These critics have never generated an original idea. All they do is mouth the dogmas handed down to them by their teachers. These teachers are of the kind criticized by Jean-Paul Sartre as reported in the book, *Sartre, los intelectuales y la política*:

> A university professor is almost always—and the same was the case in my time—a man who has written a thesis and spends the rest of his life defending it. He is furthermore a person who holds a power to which he is fiercely attached: that of imposing on others, in the name of the knowledge he has acquired, his own ideas, without giving his students the right to discuss them.(52-53, my translation)

The Expert Witness's virulent attack on the standing of the West Indian intellectual is a perfect example of the unimaginative, mindless defender of the "faith" approach. True to his mandate, the Expert Witness determined that the West Indian intellectual was obsessed with proving that Kemet was THE source of all civilization. He dismissed his work as a version of "fantasy history," as that of a dreamer obsessed with the past glories of ancient Egypt, but failing to attend to the harsh realities of the present. For the minions of Eurocentricism, the harsh realities are exclusively the self-destructive, self-hating behaviors exhibited by Africans in the continent of Africa and throughout the globe.

The Expert Witness and the other critics of Afrocentricism have missed the point. Afrocentric scholars study ancient Africa not to wallow in nostalgia, but with the understanding that a people who do not know from whence they came will never know where they are headed. Afrocentric scholars know what all true intellectuals (in the sense presented by Sartre) know: namely that unless human beings know the past they are doomed to repeat the errors of their ancestors. Afrocentric scholars, urged by Cheikh Anta Diop, study Egypt so that they can devise the road map out of white supremacy.

Nehusi, for example, has committed himself to mastering the classical language of humanity, Middle Egyptian, commonly known as simply the hieroglyphs. This knowledge of the language and culture of Middle Egyptian has prepared Nehusi to undertake an impressive study of the educational system developed by his glorious ancestors. Only a fool or a person blinded by greed or hatred would characterize Nehusi's work as empty glorification of past greatness. The Expert Witness put pen to paper to characterize Nehusi's work in the area of Carnival precisely as that, empty glorification of past greatness. He did so when he dismissed the book on Carnival co-edited by Smart and Nehusi.

As West Indian intellectuals and, indeed, all intellectuals face the complexities of introducing Affirmative Action into higher education, it is extremely useful to consider Nehusi's research on the educational system developed by the people who created civilization. Nehusi reports in his as yet unpublished study, "The System of Education in Kemet (Ancient Egypt)," that there clearly "was an elaborate and sophisticated terminology for articulating the realities of a mature education system which was conscious of itself." He reaches the "inescapable conclusion ... that the Kemites had developed a clearly distinguishable system of education." Nehusi further affirms:

> The temple with its attached 'House of Life' was the site of the highest level of the *Kmt* education system. Here students were expected to master both the Ten Virtues and the Seven Liberal Arts and were consequently graded upon their attainment in both 'moral efficiency and intellectual competence.' ... The universal aim of education was the maintainance of *Ma'at*: Justice, Righteousness, Balance, Truth—indeed cosmic harmony for which the king was responsible but in which everyone played a part by knowing and doing *Ma'at* and keeping *Isfet* (its opposite) at bay.

Nehusi faithfully acknowledges that his own work stands on the shoulders of the research of Jacob H. Carruthers, Théophile Obenga, Maulana Karenga, and others. He provides the following conclusion to his important, though as yet unpublished study:

> The evidence indicates that the Ancient Egyptians evolved a system of education which is clearly indicated by an elaborate and sophisticated terminology. This system had a number of principles and features including grading of students, grading of learning tasks

according to difficulty levels, a degree of specialization of learning institutions, location of the learner in the environment and within the world of work, location of the learner at the center of learning, mentoring by masters and mental and physical discipline. This was a system conscious of itself as an agent for the transformation of the individual student as well as the society.

In response to an initiative of the dean of the Graduate School of Arts and Sciences of the Capstone, the West Indian intellectual made specific proposals for taking the Department of Modern Languages and Literatures to tier-one status. The proposal was formulated as a five-year plan and would require the immediate implementation of certain measures.

The first measure was the reinstatement of the doctoral program in Spanish and French. This program had been inaugurated with much fanfare in 1978. Three years later, when the West Indian intellectual was appointed to serve as director of the graduate program of his department, the Graduate School of Arts and Sciences had already begun to talk about terminating the Ph.D. programs in French and Spanish. The leadership at the Capstone had apparently realized that the interests of the white supremacist mainstream Academy would not be advanced by having a thriving doctoral program in Romance Languages at a "Negro" college.

The second measure for immediate implementation was the reconfiguration of course offerings in Spanish so that the entire program would, in fact, be African centered. Thus the area "Afro-Hispanic" would be removed, since all course offerings would be based on the principle that the subject area would be Hispanophone Africana Studies. Peninsular and Latin American, the two major areas, will remain. They would now be seen as the principal branches of the overarching subject, Hispanophone Africana

Studies.

The Department is currently under the control of faculty members who are happy with the status quo and who had persuaded the Capstone to allow them to hire three new tenure track faculty members in Spanish. It would have been counterproductive to proceed with these plans, which would have ensured the continuation of the current program. On the other hand, within one year the Department should have in place a viable system of graduate teaching assistants. There should be no fewer than twelve such in Spanish, who would teach the bulk of the intermediate level language courses. It is important that the most senior faculty members teach the beginning level language courses. As is the practice in the mainstream Academy, the teaching assistants would be the core population of the graduate program.

With a Ph.D. program in Spanish (understood as Hispanophone Africana Studies), the Department could proceed to recruit graduate students nationwide and globally. A program in Hispanophone Africana Studies will be unique and consequently very attractive. The majority of the faculty in the Department is tenured, so it will be advisable to invite all of the current faculty, regardless of their present areas of concentration, to present new or modified courses to fit the new focus.

"Affirmative Action" and "West Indian Intellectual" Properly Understood

In the section, "The Limits of the Affirmative Action Program," of chapter 2, it was pointed out that this specific Program has to be a transitional entity. When African Americans are no longer burdened with the sad legacy of the trans-Atlantic slave trade, chattel slavery, and unrelenting institutionalized racism, the Affirmative Action Program instituted by the federal government in response to the Civil Rights Movement will have achieved its end. This end is exactly coterminous with the self-empowerment of Africans globally. In the terms of Marcus Garvey, Africans will become what they once used to be. It cannot be overstated that a condition sine qua non for the achievement of this goal is complete knowledge of precisely what Africans used to be. Hence the fundamental importance of the branch of study that has come to be labeled Afrocentricism.

The attentive reader will by this point have become aware that a West Indian intellectual is by definition an Afrocentric intellectual. Afrocentrism is not just another form of unhealthy ethnocentrism. Every human being is defined by her/his specific cultural experience. Humanity exists only as a concept. Warm, breathing individual human beings, a total of six billion so far, are what we encounter, not "humanity." Each human being is unique and that uniqueness is mediated through the individual's integration into a particular cultural tradition. There are many different cultural traditions, but they can all be subsumed under three main headings, namely, the African, the Asiatic, and the European.

These headings or groups correspond to the three main divisions of the one human race. Race is ultimately a theoretical construct, since there is only one human race. However, intellection itself, not to mention any form of hermeneutics, would be impossible without theoretical constructs. The theoretical construct of race is, then, a necessary evil.

Since each individual is centered in some specific cultural heritage, and since each individual belongs to one of the three main racial groups, it follows that under normal circumstances every individual's centering cultural heritage would correspond to her/his racial identification. It is normal, then, that a person who is of the European race be centered in some one of the many European cultural traditions. It is normal, then, that a person who is of the African race be centered in some one of the many African cultural traditions. It is normal, then, that a person who is of the Asiatic race be centered in some one of the many Asiatic cultural traditions.

In all human affairs, "the exception proves the rule." The problem arises when the exception becomes the rule. It is an incontrovertible fact that European ethnocentrism is founded on making the exception into the rule. For European ethnocentrism seeks to have every human being centered in a European cultural tradition. At the end of the eighteenth century European intellectuals created white supremacy, a carefully conceived system to ensure total economic control of the world by Europeans. White supremacy was founded through what Martin Bernal terms "The Fabrication of Ancient Greece" on the "Aryan Model."

Afrocentrism stands in fundamental opposition to the unhealthy ethnocentrism, which is white supremacy. There are probably as many forms of Afrocentrism as there are Africans. However, since it is possible to distinguish three main sets of cultural traditions which correspond generally to the three main "races" into which all human beings are divided, it follows that all forms of Afrocentricm would fit into the overarching category.

Individuals of African descent are native to every region of the globe. It is reasonable to refer to all of these individuals as Africans. Africans born in the Anglophone Caribbean are culturally different from Africans who were born in North America, or Africans who were born in South America, or Africans who were born in Europe, or Africans who were born in Africa, or Africans who were born in Asia. These differences are, however, outweighed by the fundamental similarities which exist between the many different African cultural traditions. On the basis of these similarities, it is reasonable to posit the existence of ONE African cultural tradition.

It was indicated in the introduction that the term "West Indian" was chosen for the purpose of signifying, of drawing attention to the significant problems its use presents. Ultimately, there are no West Indians, no African Americans, no Afro-Antillean Panamanians, no foreign Blacks, just Africans who happen to have been born in different regions of the globe. Recognition of this reality is one of the major steps towards complying with the Bob Marley injunction: "Emancipate yourselves from mental slavery."

The Frederick Douglass Road Map

The Expert Witness, in chapter four, was compared to Edward Covey, the Negro Breaker. In his *Life and Times of Frederick Douglass*, the author recounts his experiences with Covey. He had been sent to Covey's farm to be broken in. After six months of repeated whippings at the hands of the brutal white man, one Sunday morning Douglass found "the daring spirit necessary to grapple with a man who, eight-and-forty hours before, could, with his slightest word, have made me tremble like a leaf in a storm" (140). Douglass's resistance is limited to defending himself. However, when Covey enlists the help of his cousin, Hughes, the strategy changes. "I was still defensive toward Covey, but aggressive toward Hughes, on whom, at his first approach, I dealt a blow which fairly sickened him" (140-41).

Hughes withdrew forthwith from the fray. Covey next tried to enlist the support of Bill, an enslaved African who was merely hired out to Covey. Douglass recounts: "The scene here had something comic about it. Bill, who knew precisely what Covey wished him to do, affected ignorance, and pretended he did not know what to do." When finally confronted with Covey's direct command to render assistance in the whipping of the sixteen-year-old, "Bill replied, with spirit, 'My master hired me here to work, and not to help you whip Frederick.' ... Bill walked off, leaving Covey and myself to settle our differences as best we might."

Douglass continues his remarkable account as follows:

> But my present advantage was threatened when I saw Caroline (the slave woman of Covey) coming to the cow-yard to milk, for she was a powerful woman, and could have mastered me easily, exhausted as I was.
>
> As soon as she came near, Covey attempted to rally her to his aid. Strangely and fortunately, Caroline was in no humor to take a hand in any such sport. We were all in open rebellion that morning. Caroline answered the command of her master to "take hold of me," precisely as Bill had done, but in her it was at far greater peril, for she was the slave of Covey, and he could do what he pleased with her. It was not so with Bill, and Bill knew it. (141-42)

O, what a glorious Sunday morning that was for all Africans! What a wonderful example of self-affirmation! As Douglass's narrative will make clear self-affirmation is the sufficient condition for emancipation from mental slavery, and, in his case, only a necessary condition for emancipation from physical slavery.

> At length (two hours had elapsed) the contest was given over. . . . The fact was, he had not whipped me at all. He had not, in all the

> scuffle, drawn a single drop of blood from me. I had drawn blood from him . . . .
>
> During the whole six months that I lived with Covey after this transaction, he never again laid the weight of his finger on me in anger. . . .
>
> This battle with Mr. Covey . . . was the turning-point in my "life as a slave." It rekindled in my breast the smouldering embers of liberty. It brought up my Baltimore dreams and revived a sense of my own manhood. (142-43)

For Sartre, for Socrates, for KRS-ONE, manhood comes from questioning. For Douglass, the enslaved African, manhood comes from self-affirmation.

> I was a changed being after that fight. I was nothing before—I was a man now. It recalled to life my crushed self-respect, and my self-confidence, and inspired me with a renewed determination to be a free man. A man without force is without the essential dignity of humanity. (143)

It is no wonder that the Expert Witness, the contemporary incarnation of Edward Covey, was so intensely hostile to the West Indian intellectual's self-publishing. He recognized it as the most effective form of self-affirmation for the nonwhite, and hence the most dangerous threat to affirmative action as white male privilege.

Douglass declares with illuminating force:

> Covey was a tyrant and a cowardly one withal. After resisting him, I felt as I had never felt before. It was a resurrection from the dark and pestiferous tomb of slavery, to the heaven of comparative freedom. I was no longer a servile coward, trembling under the frown of a brother worm of the dust, but my long-cowed spirit was

> roused to an attitude of independence. I had reached the point at which I was *not afraid to die*. This spirit made me a freeman in *fact*, though I still remained a slave in *form*. (143)

Legal enslavement, slavery in *form* as Douglass termed it, ended in the nineteenth century. Mental slavery continues. Ironically, many Africans and other nonwhites find themselves freemen in *form*, though enslaved in *fact* by mental slavery. The Capstone of Negro Education is an institution which is supposed to effect the emancipation of African Americans from the physical plantation. However, it has become a veritable mental plantation. This book has argued that whereas the Affirmative Action Program in higher education should be the primary mechanism for effecting the liberation from mental slavery, it functions in exactly the opposite fashion. It perpetuates mental slavery. This book has presented a road map—one of many, to be sure—to liberation. It is essentially the same road map followed by Frederick Douglass. It is available to all human beings.

REFERENCES

Allen, James P. *Middle Egyptian: An Introduction to the Language and Culture of Hieroglyphs*. Cambridge: Cambridge University Press, 2000.

Bernal, Martin. *Black Athena: The Afroasiatic Roots of Classical Civilization*. 2 vols. New Brunswick, New Jersey: Rutgers University Press, 1987, 1991.

Camus, Albert. *La Peste*. Paris: Gallimard, 1947.

Césaire, Aimé. *Cahier d'un retour au pays natal / Return to My Native Land*. Trans. Emile Snyder. Paris: Présence Africaine, 1971.

Cyrus, Stanley. *El cuento negrista sudamericano: Antología*. Quito: Casa de la Cultura Ecuatoriana, 1973.

Diop, Cheikh Anta. *Civilization or Barbarism: An Authentic Anthropology*. Trans. Yaa-Lengi Meema Ngemi. Eds. Harold J. Salemson and Marjolijn de Jager. New York: Hill, 1991.

_____. *The African Origin of Civilization: Myth or Reality*. Ed. and trans. Mercer Cook. New York: Hill, 1974.

Dawkins-Smart, Buena Isidra. "The Conflict-Replacement and Flexibility-Synthesis Models Relative to Language Attitudes and Language Choices of a Panamanian Minority Group." M.A. Paper. UCLA, 1980.

Douglass, Frederick. 1892. *Life and Times of Frederick Douglass Written by Himself.* Reprint. and rev. New York: Collier, 1962.

Duncan, Quince and Carlos Meléndez, eds. *El negro en Costa Rica*. 5th ed. San José: Editorial Costa Rica, 1978.

Echeverría, Bolívar and Carlos Castro. Eds. and trans. *Sartre, los intelectuales y la política*. Mexico City: Siglo XXI, 1968.

Fanon, Frantz. *The Wretched of the Earth.* Trans. Constance Farrington. Suffolk: Penguin, 1970.

Felder, Cain H. *Troubling Biblical Waters: Race, Class, and Family.* Maryknoll, New York: Orbis Books, 1989.

Finch, Charles S. *Echoes of the Old Darkland: Themes from the African Eden.* Decatur, Georgia: Khenti, 1991.

Flores, Justin. *The Garifuna Story Now and Then.* California: n.p., 1979.

Gardiner Davenport, Frances, ed. *European Treaties Bearing on the History of the United States and Its Dependencies to 1648.* 1917. Gloucester, Mass.: Peter Smith, 1967.

García, Jorge J. E. and Mireya Camurati. Eds. *Philosophy and Literature in Latin America: A Critical Assessment of the Current Situation.* Albany: SUNY Press, 1989.

Gates, Henry Louis, *The Signifying Monkey: A Theory of African-American Literary Criticism.* New York: Oxford University Press, 1988.

Grégoire, Henri. *An Enquiry Concerning the Intellectual and Moral Faculties and Literature of Negroes: Followed with an Account of the Life and Works of Fifteen Negroes and Mulattoes Distinguished in Science, Literature and the Arts.* Trans. D. B. Warden. Brooklyn, 1810. Reprint. College Park, Maryland: McGrath Publishing Company, 1967.

Griaule, Marcel. *Conversations with Ogotemmêli: An Introduction to Dogon Religious Ideas.* London: Oxford University Press, 1965.

Herdeck, Donald E. et al. Eds. *Caribbean Writers: A Bio-Bibliographical-Critical Encyclopedia.* Washington, D.C.: Three Continents Press, 1979.

Hilliard, Asa G., Larry Williams, and Nia Damali, eds. *The Teachings of Ptahhotep: The Oldest Book in the World.* Atlanta: Blackwood Press, 1987.

Hughes, Langston. *Selected Poems.* New York: Vintage, 1974.

Hull, Gloria T. *Color, Sex, and Poetry: Three Women Writers of the Harlem Renaissance.* Bloomington: Indiana University Press, 1987.

Jackson, John G. *Introduction to African Civilizations.* 2nd ed. Secaucus, New Jersey: The Citadel Press, 1974.

James, C. L. R. *The Black Jacobins: Toussaint L'Ouverture and the San Domingo Revolution.* 2nd ed. rev. New York: Vintage Books, 1963.

James, George G. M. *Stolen Legacy: The Greeks were not the authors of Greek Philosophy, but the people of North Africa, commonly called the Egyptians.* 1954. Reprint. San Francisco: Julian Richardson Associates, 1985.

Jefferson, Thomas. *Notes on a State of Virginia.* Ed. William Peden. Chapel Hill: University of North Carolina Press, 1982.

KRS-ONE, *Ruminations.* New York: Welcome Rain Publishers, 2003.

Lewis, Lancelot S. *The West Indian in Panama: Black Labor in Panama, 1850-1914.* Washington, D.C.: University Press of the Americas, 1980.

Liverpool, Hollis "Chalkdust." *Rituals of Power and Rebellion: The Carnival Tradition in Trinidad and Tobago 1763-1962.* Chicago: Frontline Distribution Int'l, 2001.

Logan, Paul E., ed. *A Howard Reader: An Intellectual and Cultural Quilt of the African-American Experience.* Boston: Houghton Mifflin, 1997.

Lowe-Ocran, Melva. "El idioma inglés y la integración social de los panameños de origen afro-antillano al carácter nacional panameño." *Revista Nacional de Cultura* 5 (1976): 22-43.

Maloney, Gerardo. *Juega vivo.* Panamá: Ediciones Formato Dieciséis, 1984.

Malraux, André. *La condition humaine.* Paris: Gallimard, 1946.

Morejón, Nancy. *Recopilación de textos sobre Nicolás Guillén.* La Habana: Casa de las Américas, 1974.

Morton, Allen G. "The Private Schools of the British West Indians in Panama." Diss. George Peabody College for Teachers, 1966.

Naipaul, V. S. *The Middle Passage: The Caribbean Revisited.* 2nd ed.Middlesex: Penguin Books, 1969.

Pascal, Blaise. *Pensées.* 1670. Paris: Le Livre de Poche, 1962.

Racine, Daniel, ed. *Léon-Gontran Damas, 1912-1978: Founder of Negritude A Memorial Casebook.* Washington, D.C.: University Press of America, 1979.

_____. *Léon-Gontran Damas: L'homme et l'oeuvre.* Paris:Présence Africaine, 1983.

Ramírez, Manuel. "Recognizing and Understanding Diversity: Multiculturalism and the Chicano Movement in Psychology." *Chicano Psychology.* Ed. Joe L. Martínez, Jr. New York: Academic Press, 1977. 343-53.

Rohlehr, Gordon. *Calypso & Society in Pre-Independence Trinidad.* Port-of-Spain: Gordon Rohlehr, 1990.

_____. *Pathfinder: Black Awakening in* The Arrivants *of Edward Kamau Brathwaite.* Tunapuna, Trinidad and Tobago: Gordon Rohlehr, 1981.

Roumain, Jacques. *Masters of the Dew.* Trans. Langston Hughes and Mercer Cook. New York: Collier 1971.

Rout, Leslie B., Jr. *The African Experience in Spanish America: 1502 to the Present Day.* Cambridge: Cambridge University Press, 1976.

Senghor, Léopold Sédar. Ed. *Anthologie de la nouvelle poésie nègre et malgache de langue française.* 3rd ed. Paris: Presses Unveri-sitaires de France, 1972.

Smart, Ian Isidore. *Amazing Connections: Kemet to Hispanophone Africana Literature.* Washington, D.C.: Original World Press, 1996.

_____. *Central American Writers of West Indian Origin: A New Hispanic Literature.* Washington, D.C.: Three Continents Press, 1984.

_____. *Spoiled Priest.* Washington, D.C.: Original World Press, 2002.

_____. "The *Afro-Hispanic Reivew.*" *Philosophy and Literature in Latin America: A Critical Assessment of the Current Situation.* Eds. Jorge J. E. García and Mireya Camurati. Albany: SUNY Press, 1989. 194-200.

_____. "West Indian Whispers from Central America." *The Western Journal of Black Studies* 17 (1993): 103-11.

Taylor, Douglas M. *The Black Carib of British Honduras*. New York: Wenner-Green Foundation, 1951.

Thomas, J. J. *The Theory and Practice of Creole Grammar*. 1869. Reprint. London: New Beacon Books, 1969.

Trotman, David Vincent. *Crime in Trinidad: Conflict and Control in a Plantation Society, 1838-1900*. Knoxville: University of Tennessee Press, 1986.

Van Sertima, Ivan. *They Came Before Columbus: The African Presence in Ancient America*. New York: Random House, 1976.

Welch, Winston R. "Evolución de la población negroide en Panamá." Unpublished paper.

Woodson, Carter G. *The Mis-Education of the Negro*. 1933. Reprint. Trenton: Africa World Press, 1990.

Williams, Chancellor. *The Destruction of Black Civilization: Great Issues of a Race from 4500 B.C. to 2000 A.D.* Chicago: Third World Press, 1976.

Williams, Eric. *Capitalism and Slavery*. 2nd ed. New York: Capricon Books, 1966.

Zapata Olivella, Manuel. *Las claves mágicas de América*. Bogota: Plaza y Janes, 1989.

Index

Index

Index

Index

Index